Advance Praise for Tribal Warri(

"The phenomenal expansion of our culturally diverse population in the United States is presenting both challenges and opportunities in our interactions, learning and work experiences. Considering that within 50 years nearly half of the nation's population will be from cultures other than White non-Hispanic, the need to have the appropriate tools to navigate this new reality has become more than just compelling. Understanding ourselves and others in a more comprehensive approach is today's key to success."

"Knowing how to navigate this new system without prejudice, isolation or alienation will make our lives richer and exciting. The tools and concepts presented in this book achieve the goal to guide us into the journey of getting out of our own shell."

—Kay Itzigsohn, MA, LPC

"A teenager's world can be filled with bullies, addiction, violence, early sexualization, adolescent angst, and various other pitfalls. *Tribal Warriors* is a ray of hope for parents, schools, and communities. It gathers constructive gems from world cultures and delineates a clear path to developing confident, optimistic, nurturing, productive and protective youth. In short, young people who are more likely to grow into strong, self-assured and valuable members of their communities. For all the adults who lament the lack of a book of instructions for raising upright children, there is now *Tribal Warriors*. And for those who believe they have the child-rearing formula down pat, make no mistake, *Tribal Warriors* will nourish your knowledge. In today's world, no one can afford to ignore *Tribal Warriors*."

—Dr. Shamita Das Dasgupta, PhD

"Our culture is changing rapidly while simultaneously our young people are longing for true community. Our children are at risk of a low grade chronic trauma induced by the pervasiveness of media and messages that do not promote healthy social relationship and emotionally satisfying connections. Prevention against this is needed at a young age as it is much more difficult to correct these effects later in life.

Tribal Warriors offers a multimodality approach to build a solid foundation of inner wealth based on the strength of diversity while celebrating our true nature of interdependence. In *Tribal Warriors*, young people are given tools to master social relationships based on valuing all and navigating from a strong sense of their worth and the worth of others."

—Jamie Gregory, MSW, LICSW

Advance Praise for Tribal Warriors

"In my work as a physician I have seen the amazing results of the Nurtured Heart Approach® on an individual and family level for many years. However, I have often thought about how much more effective this approach could be if it was applied at the school and community level by teaching youth how to use the approach among themselves. *Tribal Warriors* is our guide to doing just that. The Nurtured Heart Approach® is presented as the overarching approach in this integrated model that increases overall well-being. It is a how-to workbook that will enable schools and other community groups to help students and clients to overcome the great difficulties inherent in our social and educational system, and thrive to their fullest potential. I would recommend this book to anyone interested in the education, development, and success of our children."

—Dr. Sanford Newmark, Head of the Pediatric Integrative Neurodevelopmental Clinic, Osher Center for Integrative Medicine, University of California, San Francisco

TRIBAL WARRIORS:
Life Skills to Optimize Well-Being for Teens

"The creatively painted artwork was provided with great compassion and support for the concept of encouraging a shift back to our tribal roots. I was very blessed to have journeyed for a short while with Mr. Somerville and his family. His daughter, Heather, embellished his painting with her amazingly gifted talent as a photographer. We are deeply grateful for their contribution to this project."

—Sherry A. Blair

A Message from the Artist Whom Created the *Tribal Warriors* Book Cover

Kia ora:

I am a Māori descendant from the Nga-i Tahu tribes of the southern regions of New Zealand. I am both Scottish and Mori. The Artist, Sydney Parkinson sailed with Captain James Cook when he landed in this idyllic environment. He did drawings and studies of the Māori people and fauna of the New Zealand landscape. I am a painter and artist I have painted for many years. My inspiration is derived from the oceans of the southwestern pacific. The Māori images in my art are influenced by both Modern Abstract Expression and traditional native images.

Tribal communities are very important for the stability of our youth. They are the relationships handed down from our tribal elders. The passing of these traditions have a profound influence on family and respect for wise council. I try to achieve a spiritual bridge of understanding and compassion in a world fractionated in pain.

—Thomas Somerville, taokumite@yahoo.com

Sherry A. Blair

TRIBAL WARRIORS:
Life Skills to Optimize Well-Being for Teens

An Integrated Model Creating Nurtured Heart® Communities

www.tribalwarriorsblog.com

Cover Design by: Thomas Somerville,
Heather Somerville, and Kristine Requena

Character Illustrations by: Brenda Brown
www.webtoon.com

Graphics and Page Layout by: Kristine Requena
www.getGraphic.net

ISBN-10: 1477462643
ISBN-13: 978-1477462645

Table of Contents

Table of Contents

The Heat is On: The Nurtured Heart Approach®

Your Body: What's Food & Activity Got to Do with It?

Make These Deposits Daily

We began with you, & you are on your way to transforming. **NOW**-time to change the world!

SECTION TWO: Tribal Warriors Stand Against Violence, Hate Crimes & Bullying in Schools & Communities. Tribal Warriors STAND for Positivity, Respect & Compassion Toward Themselves & Others

Gratitude & Acknowledgments

I would first like to thank the children and families who have afforded me the privilege of entering their homes since the late 1990s. This work would be meaningless without having had these experiences. I am also grateful to all the individual adults who used these tools throughout the years. Because of this I was inspired to "translate" all this information for middle and high school youth, realizing how important it is to develop these skills before adulthood.

Secondly, I am very blessed to work with such a committed group of outstanding human beings who believe in my leadership and have stayed with ISIS throughout the years and through the ups and downs associated with a small business and its growing pains. I would especially like to thank Connie Masullo, Brendaly Sanchez-Abarca, Toni Anne Lofrano, Nancy Azevedo-Bonilla, Erica LeFurge, Phil Hymowitz, Marianne Rubino, and Marcela Kepicova. In addition, I thank all of you who have recently come on board because you are attracted to our passion for service and the philosophy to which we subscribe. To all of you who have come and gone through the years, I am grateful for your servitude and what you have contributed to New Jersey's Wraparound System of Care through our in-home program. Without you the ISIS in-home program would not exist.

Many thanks to our system partners in New Jersey who have supported the work we do and continue to notice that ISIS is not only doing something different but also upholds quality standards for care. Thank you to Partnership for Children of Essex, Hudson Partnership, Caring Partners of Morris & Sussex, Circle of Care for Children and Families of Passaic County, Bergen's Promise, Families And Children Together, and Coordinated Family Care. Thank you to Essex, Passaic, and Union Mobile Response and Stabilization Services and the past leaders and staff at Youth Case Management of Bergen, Essex, Hudson, Middlesex, Morris, Passaic, Sussex, and Union Counties. Additional thanks to Tri-County Care Management Organization for recently inviting us to serve in Hunterdon, Warren, and Somerset Counties.

Sincere gratitude and "gratefulness" go to Dr. Martin Seligman who energized the modern day positive psychology movement. The plethora of research and practice that has emerged for more than a decade is changing lives for the better. Dr. Barbara Fredrickson, Dr. Sonja Lyubomirsky, and Dr. Mihaly Csikszentmihalyi are all to be commended for the brilliant work you are doing in this movement. You have influenced and inspired me in my work. Thank you for proving that optimizing people in life toward positivity, flow, and happiness is one of the most valuable things you can do.

The camaraderie found in the Nurtured Heart Approach® (NHA) world has been a pulse of positivity in both my personal and professional lives since 2008 when I was gifted with the knowledge of this approach from my then supervisee, Connie Masullo. Since that time ISIS has taken the approach to be a part of our special branding along with positive psychology interventions, and we have used the approach as the thread that binds all of our work together in an effort to accelerate flourishing in the lives of the people we serve.

Howard "Howie" Glasser, you are the one who trusted your intuition and skillfully created these precision tools and nurturing style for using language that are changing lives all around the world in homes, schools, families, communities, and workplaces. Thank you for your vision and persistence to spread the word of this life changing approach.

Lisa Bravo, you have creatively taken the Nurtured Heart Approach® and applied it in both your personal and professional lives to become the first master trainer of the approach. We at ISIS are indebted to you for sharing your creativity in the application of the approach to help us better serve children and families in New Jersey. Your clinical consultations offer us invaluable insight and inspiration and we all thank you and appreciate your "out of the box" application.

I am humbled and blessed to have developed amazing and longstanding relationships with Nurtured Heart Approach® Advanced Trainers and especially would like to honor the following people for past and present collaboration: Joe Clem, Alletta Bayer, BJ Byrd, Sarah Howe, Tanya Frazier, Jan Hunter, Angie Smith, Jim Kimberling, Laura Montané-Bailey, Melissa Lynn Block, Celeste Elsey, Catherine Stafford, Jamie Gregory, Nechama Tarlow, Peggy Archuleta, Pam Harsacky, Tim and Pat Bethke, and Sandy Newmark.

I am so truly honored and grateful to the contributors listed below who took precious time out of your extremely busy lives to peruse this manuscript and provide solid feedback and endorsement for the use of *Tribal Warriors*.

Kay Birnbaun-Itzigsohn, MA
Cultural Diversity Consultant

Kay Itzigsohn, MA, LPC is the former Director of the Survivors of War Trauma and Torture Program at the International Institute of New Jersey where she provided mental health treatment, training, and clinical supervision for survivors from Africa, Asia, the Middle East, Europe, the Former Soviet Union, and Latin America. Earlier, she was a clinician for the 9/11 Program at the Institute.

Prior to working at the International Institute of New Jersey, Ms. Itzigsohn spent 15 years as a clinician for survivors of psychological trauma in Israel, including five years as the in-house psychologist with the National Transportation Company where she responded in the aftermath of terrorist attacks on buses. While in Israel, she also served as a school psychologist and a clinical psychologist.

Her training includes family and marital therapy, personality disorders, learning disabilities, and specialized training in working with trauma, including eye movement desensitization and reprocessing (EMDR). She is currently a candidate at the New Jersey Institute for Training in Psychoanalysis. She has presented papers at the International Society of Traumatic Stress Studies World Conference in Buenos Aires, Argentina and at the Immigration and Trauma Conference in Israel. She was raised in Buenos Aires where she received her master's degree in Clinical Psychology from Belgrano University and worked as a human rights activist in the aftermath of the military government.

She was also a board member of the Bergen County Sanctuary Committee, an interfaith organization that fights for the reform of the asylum process and serves as a sponsor for asylum seekers who are in federal detention centers for immigrants. She worked in private practice at a low cost clinic in New Jersey. For several years she trained mental health clinicians and administrators in Cultural Competence, a program funded by the New Jersey Division of Mental Health and sponsored by the International Institute of New Jersey and the Mental Health Association in New Jersey. Kay now lives in Israel where she is practicing as a psychologist in a day program and developing an intense psychotherapeutic program for victims of sexual abuse. She is serving children and families struggling with challenges related to developmental disabilities and immigration.

BJ Byrd, MS
Certified Nurtured Heart Approach® Specialist

BJ Byrd, BS, MS earned her bachelor's degree from the University of California at Davis (1990) and her master's degree from the University of Colorado at Boulder (1993). In 2000, she went back to school to become a teacher earning her certification from California State University at Hayward. BJ Byrd has been a physical education teacher for the past 13 years in the San Ramon Valley Unified School District. For the past three years, she has motivated and encouraged her elementary school students to achieve the title of Presidential Physical Fitness State Champions (2010 and 2011). Mrs. Byrd lives with her partner and their six year old son in the East Bay Area. BJ Byrd is an Advanced Trainer/Certified Nurtured Heart Approach® Specialist.

Carly Mentlik

Carly Mentlik is a Licensed Professional Clinical Counselor, Registered Yoga Teacher and Certified Special Education Teacher. She is the founder and owner of Mandala Learning, a small business offering holistic counseling and learning support services for children through adults. Carly has been working with children, teens and families as a teacher, counselor and mentor for over 14 years. She received her Bachelor's degree in Special Education and Master's degree in Counseling from New York University. During her graduate studies, she worked on a research team that extensively studied adolescent development and interviewed teens about their experiences in friendships and romantic relationships. Since that time, she has continued to develop her knowledge by completing trainings in Prana Flow Yoga, Reiki and the Nurtured Heart Approach®. Carly has recently developed a unique learning approach that aims to give areas such as personal development, creative thinking and community learning as much importance as has traditionally been afforded solely to academics.

Shamita Das DasGupta, PhD
Manavi Co-Founder

Shamita Das DasGupta is a co-founder of Manavi (New Jersey), the first organization in the United States to focus on violence against South Asian immigrant women. She has been engaged in advocacy to end violence against women for over 30 years. Shamita Das DasGupta is currently teaching as an adjunct professor at New York University School of Law. In addition to several articles and reports, she is the author of the following four books—*The Demon Slayers and Other Stories: Bengali Folktales* (1995, Interlink Books, USA); *A Patchwork Shawl: Chronicles of South Asian Women in America* (1998, Rutgers University Press, USA); *Body Evidence: Intimate Violence Against South Asian Women in America (2007, Rutgers University Press, USA); and Mothers for Sale: Women in Kolkata's Sex Trade* (2009, DasGupta-Alliance, India). Shamita Das DasGupta currently serves on several national boards. Since 2000, she has been appointed by New Jersey's Governor to the New Jersey Domestic Violence Fatality and Near Fatality Review Board. In addition to various awards, her work has received wide recognition in national and international media.

Celeste Elsey, MA
Certified Nurtured Heart Approach® Specialist

Celeste Elsey, MA is a resource teacher in the Special Education Department at Cooley Middle School in Roseville, California and is a Nurtured Heart Approach® Advanced Trainer. She uses the Nurtured Heart Approach® daily with her students. She also trains Academic Peer Mentors (Greatness Kids) in the approach and teaches the Nurtured Heart Approach® classes to parents and educators. Celeste Elsey lives in Roseville with her husband Joe and their three sons Michael, Tyler, and Jordan.

Jamie Gregory, MSW, LICSW
Certified Nurtured Heart Approach® Specialist

James "Jamie" Gregory is a Licensed Independent Clinical Social Worker in private practice in Charles Town, West Virginia. His background is brain-based and heart-centered with a strengths-perspective and solution-focused orientation to therapy. He is a Certified Practitioner of Neuro-Linguistic Programming (NLP) and a Nurtured Heart

Approach® Specialist. He serves on his local Children's Advocacy Center (CAC) Multi-Disciplinary Team reviewing and assessing all reported cases of child physical and sexual abuse in the county where he resides. He has training in Trauma-Focused Cognitive Behavioral Therapy (TFCBT).

Mr. Gregory also teaches as an adjunct faculty professor in the Graduate Program of Social Work at West Virginia University. In addition, he teaches a Family Strengthening series based on the Nurtured Heart Approach® 24 weeks of the year. He also serves as a consultant to the Head Start Program.

He practices Heart Rhythm Mediation, plays guitar, and sings in a musical trio. He loves to garden, bird watch, and kayak, and he lives with his beloved wife, Nancy, in a passive solar house they built 26 years ago in the Shenandoah River Valley of West Virginia. They have two sons, Jay, 31 and Seth, 24.

Toni Anne Lofrano, BA
NHA Trained/NJ State Certified Behavioral Assistant, ISIS Positivity Pulse Specialist, Content Editor

Toni Anne Lofrano received her Bachelor's Degree in Child Advocacy with minors in Psychology and Criminal Justice from Montclair State University in Montclair, New Jersey. She has 9 years of experience working as an in-home Behavioral Assistant with boys and girls between the ages of 4 and 21 who have emotional and behavioral health challenges. She has been employed at ISIS Innovative Specialists Inspirational Services, LLC for the past 8 years. Toni Anne Lofrano completed the New Jersey Children's System of Care (formerly the Division of Child Behavioral Health Services) Behavioral Assistant Training Certification in 2010. She is trained in the Nurtured Heart Approach® and has been applying the approach in both her personal and professional lives. Toni Anne Lofrano also served as a program coordinator and overnight counselor for the ISIS Weekend Respite Program and was trained in Non-Violent Crisis Intervention. In 2012, she completed the Rainbows Facilitator Training. Toni Anne Lofrano is now certified to run groups through Rainbows--an international not-for-profit organization that assists children and families who are grieving a death, divorce, or other life-altering crisis. Toni Anne Lofrano has used her education, training, and experience to transform positive change with youth and families in several New Jersey Counties, including Bergen, Essex, Passaic, Hudson, and Morris. She also inspires and energizes the staff at ISIS Innovative Specialists Inspirational Services, LLC as a Positivity Pulse Leader.

Irene Maltzan, BS
Wellness Tree, Founder/Owner

Irene Maltzan is a Nutritional Counselor certified by the Institute of Integrative Nutrition and owner of the Wellness Tree. She holds a BS from Ramapo College. Irene does private nutritional counseling and teaches wellness groups specializing in family and nutritional support. She is a wellness educator that delivers seminars and presentations for corporations on holistic health. Irene has also completed her certification for nutrition at Columbia's Teachers College and is certified by the American Association of Drugless Practitioners as a holistic health counselor. She is also trained in the Nurtured Heart Approach.® Irene works with ISIS Innovative Specialists Inspirational Services, LLC to deliver wellness services to families with children who have emotional and behavioral health challenges in New Jersey's Wraparound System of Care. She has a private practice at the New Jersey Center for Healthy Living.

Laura Montané-Bailey, MS, LMFT
Certified Nurtured Heart Approach® Specialist

Laura Montané-Bailey obtained a BS in Psychology and Health from Eastern Oregon University and a MS degree in Marital and Family Therapy from Loma Linda University. Laura has been an Advanced Trainer in the Nurtured Heart Approach® since 2008, offering family therapy and training for educators, foster staff, parents, and anyone working with children who struggle with ADHD and other conduct disorders. She has worked with foster children and teens living in group homes in Southern California along with providing therapy for individuals, children, and families in a family therapy clinic. She also served as Clinical Services Coordinator, leading the efforts to deliver a motivational, skill-building program to at-risk youth in Riverside County while offering training in the Nurtured Heart Approach® to the adults who cared for them. Although she has been involved in leadership roles in various community youth programs for many years and for the last 15 years has run small groups in church and college settings, she considers her greatest accomplishment to be having raised two children who are now responsible, productive adults. She is currently working on a project to heighten awareness of the heroic efforts of over 2 million grandparents in the United States who are raising their grandchildren. Laura is scheduled to have her first book available this summer. It is titled *Courageous Love* and offers powerful steps for grandparents and other seasoned family members raising their grandchildren and kin in a troubled world.

Kristine Requena
getGraphic, LLC, Principal Designer/Founder

Kristine Requena is principal designer and founder of getGraphic, a home-based design studio located in Plainsboro, NJ. Since its establishment in 2009, getGraphic has offered professional, cost-effective, graphic design and logo services. Over the years, promotional products, printing, and copyediting have been added to the list of creative services.

Kristine comes from a strong creative background with a degree in Applied Science Marketing Art and Design Advertising Graphics and Design. She has 18 years of real world experience and technical knowledge. Her position requires her to coordinate freelancers to meet all project requirements, manage all operational and administrative functions, collaborate with clients for project development, and to design maintaining brand consistency across multiple print and web channels.

Kristine enjoys the creative challenge, working directly with her clients, and pushing herself to produce the best work possible. Kristine is a professional who plans, analyzes and creates visual solutions.

Prologue for Professionals and Caregivers

> "Positive education is defined as education for both traditional skills and for happiness. The high prevalence worldwide of depression among young people, the small rise in life satisfaction, and the synergy between learning and positive emotion all argue that the skills for happiness should be taught in school. There is substantial evidence from well controlled studies that skills that increase resilience, positive emotion, engagement and meaning can be taught to schoolchildren."
>
> —*Positive psychology and classroom interventions by*
> *Martin E.P. Seligman, Randal M. Ernst, Jane Gillham,*
> *Karen Reivich, and Mark Linkins*

Rationale for an Integrated Model for Middle School & High School Youth

The main rationale behind creating an Integrated Model for Middle School and High School youth is to create communities and aide youth in approaching life holistically but with a strong focus on increasing human capital by increasing psychological and social capital. The concepts embodied in this workbook are applicable to all youth for overall emotional, mental, social, spiritual and physical health. Life skills are not only about how to balance a checking account, take out the garbage, have good hygiene and clean your home, to name a few. In the "real world" we need skills that optimize us in life. These include our emotional well-being, relationships and physical health. Significant research has revealed the power of Emotional Intelligence and the importance of physical health to our psychological well-being, yet many mental health professionals do not create holistic or integrated treatment plans to embody these crucial life skills. This workbook embraces three powerful interventions to create flourishing in youth: the Nurtured Heart Approach®, Rational Emotive Behavioral Therapy (REBT), and positive psychology. In addition, lessons in nutrition, physical fitness, yoga and meditation are introduced.

The Nurtured Heart Approach® Story

The Nurtured Heart Approach® (NHA) is a model for interacting with others and with ourselves in ways that support transitioning toward being optimized in life by increasing resiliency, character strengths and virtues and by learning how to manage adversity with sound decision making skill building. It works in any relationship dynamic—parent/child, teacher/student, manager/employee, therapist/client, spouse/spouse, friend/friend—to build positive perceptions and language. It can positively transform a whole organizational culture, one relationship at a time.

Prologue for Professionals and Caregivers

The Nurtured Heart Approach® was created by psychotherapist Howard Glasser. While working as a family therapist, Glasser found that his efforts to help difficult children and their families to thrive often failed. Sometimes, the methods he used—which were the methods he learned to use in his psychotherapeutic training—seemed to make matters worse. The bad behavior of already out of control children was escalating. Parents (and teachers) felt more and more helpless. And during that time, more and more children were being put on Ritalin and other drugs when therapy didn't bring the situation under control.

Glasser began to work intuitively, discarding all the techniques that didn't work to help his young patients embrace their intensity and heal from their pasts as "bad teens." Over time, he developed a series of tools that worked with even the most difficult children. Not only did these children become better behaved, they seemed *transformed*. They were just as intense and alive as ever, but they had been led into a place where they wanted to use their intensity to succeed. Parents and teachers who learned and applied the approach found that it made them much more effective at drawing children out of patterns of rule-breaking and misbehavior and into patterns of ever-increasing success and happiness. They found that the NHA helped them cultivate more positive, mutually rewarding relationships with other adults as well.

At this writing, tens of thousands of households, hundreds of schools, and even a few school systems are applying the NHA. Thousands of mental health professionals apply it to their therapy practices and their work with challenged adult and pediatric populations.

Teachers are using the NHA to increase the productivity of their frontline workers—their students. Children exposed to the NHA in the classroom come to enjoy attending school; they participate more and increase their academic success because they truly want to learn. Suspensions drop, parent-teacher conversations about negative behaviors are reduced, and student trips to the office are reduced or eliminated. In schools where the NHA is applied, teacher retention has increased.

The NHA is a proactive approach to relationships that helps to circumvent time-consuming conflicts and disciplinary actions, whether it's applied in a workplace or in a school. When it's applied in the education sector, there is often a need to increase curriculum. It enhances efficiency in the workplace too, allowing for more to be accomplished in less time by reducing interpersonal conflicts and rule-breaking.

The NHA is the umbrella method for the overarching transformational techniques that are introduced to teach youth how to apply this approach to themselves and their peers. The NHA builds children and youth up from the inside out creating flourishing and "inner wealth" that embodies character strengths, virtues and values. In turn, when organizations adopt the approach, they build environments using inner wealth, and flourishing positive relationships are the result. When used independently, this approach changes lives. However, when used conjointly with other interventions, it enhances, deepens and anchors in the positivity in a more meaningful way. We like to refer to this change process as "Miracle-Grow" in real life.

Rational Emotive Behavior Therapy

Evidenced-based Rational Emotive Behavior Therapy (REBT) teaches the tools that are required to shift toward a rational thought process, ridding us of disturbing thoughts, self-defeating behaviors and unhealthy negative emotions. It is grounded in a strong philosophical foundation as well as a commitment to the scientific method. Theoretically, REBT is the interconnectedness of thinking, feeling and behaving. Emotional distress is a direct result of a dysfunctional and maladaptive thought process.

Because this workbook is designed for all youth with or without a psychiatric diagnosis, REBT is introduced as either a therapeutic intervention or a coaching model. As REBT has evolved since the middle of the last century, many practitioners have employed it as a coaching model. Rational Emotive Behavior Coaching helps all individuals move toward unconditional self-acceptance, acceptance of others and acceptance of life in general. The A-B-C model teaches us how to replace irrational beliefs with rational alternatives resulting in healthy negative and positive emotions as well as self-enhancing and positive behaviors.

Positive Psychology

Positive psychology research stresses the significance of positive health, positive education, positive relationships, positive emotions, engagement, having meaning in life, and achievement. The modern day positive psychology movement has brought forth numerous positive outcomes under the leadership of Dr. Martin Seligman and other brilliant researchers around the world. The Penn Resiliency Program described below from the University of Pennsylvania's Positive Psychology Center has proved itself to be an effective model for increasing positive emotion and relationships, and decreasing negative beliefs that result in challenges in academic success, poor peer relations and symptoms of psychiatric disorders.

> The Penn Resiliency Program (PRP), is a group intervention for late elementary and middle school students. The curriculum teaches cognitive-behavioral and social problem-solving skills and is based in part on cognitive-behavioral theories of depression by Aaron Beck, Albert Ellis, and Martin Seligman (Abramson, Seligman, & Teasdale, 1978; Beck, 1967, 1976; Ellis, 1962). Central to PRP is Ellis' Adversity Consequences-Beliefs (ABC) model, the notion that our beliefs about events mediate their impact on our emotions and behavior. Through this model, students learn to detect inaccurate thoughts, to evaluate the accuracy

of those thoughts, and to challenge negative beliefs by considering alternative interpretations. PRP also teaches a variety of strategies that can be used for solving problems and coping with difficult situations and emotions. Students learn techniques for assertiveness, negotiation, decision-making, social problem-solving, and relaxation. The skills taught in the program can be applied to many contexts of life, including relationships with peers and family members as well as achievement in academics or other activities.

—University of Penn Positive Psychology Center

Utilization of Workbook

This workbook moves beyond life skills as we traditionally know them and steps outside of the box to get middle and high school youth optimized in life and overall well-being. Section One teaches youth how to build their personal "inner wealth" and to build the inner wealth of their peers. Continuing with flourishing and transformation, Section Two pulls the tribe together to stand against all types of bullying, hate crimes and violence in their schools and communities. It is the belief that before we can address bullying to increase peaceful relationships, we need to build up all individuals, whether they have been victimized or have offended. All youth need the information presented in this workbook in order to stand together to build peaceful Nurtured Heart® communities.

The workbook is designed to begin with Section One and move through the lessons consecutively to Section Two. However, using the activities randomly is an option but comes with a caveat. Many of the lessons request reflecting back to previous lessons which is congruent with the psychology of learning and repetition. The Nurtured Heart Approach® techniques are threaded throughout the workbook regardless of the lesson.

When used in its entirety, *Tribal Warriors* is designed be taught weekly with daily practice suggestions. For use in school and community based programs, it is suggested that Section One be taught from September through January and Section Two be taught from February through June. The goal is to create leadership in schools and communities. Youth who complete the initial training participate as peer trainers in application, put into practice and apply outside of the formal weekly sessions and move forward to assist as co-leaders in subsequent years.

Research and Evidence Based Practice

We, at ISIS Innovative Specialists Inspirational Services, LLC are committed to providing services that blend both Western teachings that adhere to quality measures and outcomes that are proven by rigorous research designs and other teachings that may be considered "informal" measures. We believe in leading from our hearts and intuition which we understand is not measurable while valuing the meaning of research and understand how it drives decisions and policy. Ultimately we believe in the uniqueness of all individuals and how the beauty of culture inspires our services.

If you are interested in participating in a research project with us, contact the author, Sherry Blair at **sherry@isisnj.us**. We value the opportunity to prove the efficacy of this program. Including, but not limited to, our research design is tailored for an integrated model to measure the efficacy of the Nurtured Heart Approach®, positive psychology interventions, Rational Emotive Behavior Therapy/Coaching and positive health and fitness.

> **"Students have the right to an educational experience in which they feel valued and respected where teachers and peers clearly and actively support their development and learning, and where they are free from fear, threats and harm. Ensuring this experience for all students should be the ultimate goal of all school initiatives."**
>
> *—Dorian Wilson, MA, Data Analysis and Research Coordinator, Safe Communities - Safe Schools, Center for the Study and Prevention of Violence, Institute of Behavioral Science, University of Colorado*

For Schools as a Bullying Prevention Program

For close to two decades, I have been personally working with children and youth in their schools, in their communities and in their homes. I have worked with both the victims and the offenders and at times have discovered that the victim is often the offender in another setting. For example, if the victim is being bullied at school, he/she may come home and bully family members—parents and/or siblings. Having had a background in domestic and family violence, my training allowed me to understand the psychological and behavioral effects on all parties involved in the deleterious cycles of abuse.

My extensive work in Women and Gender Studies through the years as a student, practitioner, educator, and as a leader in executive behavioral health services has afforded me a different lens as it relates to all the "isms" in the world that lead to oppression and the coercive nature of power and control. Breaking down the barriers of racism, homophobia, sexism, ethnocentrism, xenophobia, and ageism is required. Teaching our youth to "see" each other at the heart and soul level rather than by our differences (the color of our skin, gender, sexual orientation, etc.) is the path that is required to move us toward a more humanistic and compassionate way of relating to one another without prejudice.

Within the last decade, my organization has served close to 4,000 children and families in New Jersey's Wraparound System of Care, and the issue of bullying at home, in school and in the community is disturbingly a common thread. Because of this, we believe that building the individual's "inner wealth" and increasing the tenets of REBT, specifically Unconditional Self-Acceptance (USA) and Unconditional Acceptance of Others (UAO), are the first steps toward breaking down the cycles of abuse and bullying. This workbook is designed to "speak to" youth which allows them to develop the tools for self-help and improvement. The second step is teaching our future peacemakers how to apply these techniques in their worlds while they stand together as strong, flourishing *Tribal Warriors*.

The Utility of *Tribal Warriors*

Tribal Warriors can be used with participants individually as well as in group settings including but not limited to:

- Community and Hospital Based Mental Health Programs for Adolescents

- School Based Programs with School Social Workers, Student Assistance Counselors and School Psychologists

- After School Programs

- Intensive In-Community and In-Home Behavioral Health Services in Wraparound Programs

- Community Development Programs

- Religious Youth Based Programs

- Character Building Programs

Preface

Why *Tribal Warriors*?

The title *Tribal Warriors* can be described as a concept to pull us together for a good cause and that cause is about you, your friends, your family, your community, your neighborhoods and your school. What really struck me about the word *tribal* and its etymology (which is the history of the use of a word) is the Latin connection to the word for three: *tres*. Some roots of the word are called *tribus*. The word *tribus* could therefore mean "from the three" or "for the three." What is really powerful is that it relates to some interesting things you learn in this workbook. There are three stands that you will be taking as tribal warriors that help change your life: Refuse to Energize Negativity ("Absolutely NO!"), Relentlessly Energize the Positive ("Absolutely YES!"), and Clearly and Unenergetically Enforce Limits (Absolute Clarity).

ME versus WE

By nature humans are very social beings. But something has happened along the way in the development of the United States that has interrupted our natural desire to be a *collective* or a group. We have become an *individualistic* culture meaning we think more in terms of "me" instead of "we." That is unfortunate and even sad because when people work together and strive together whether they are a family unit, a sports team, a special group, a school, a community, or a workforce they achieve much more. What is even more powerful than that is what happens within us, in our hearts, when we work together. We become truly connected and we stand up and support one another. My hope is to evoke a tribal sense within all of you that is truly part of our ancient memories. We need to awaken that part of ourselves so we can come together to make a positive change within ourselves and a positive change for the world as a whole.

One of the most important things you will learn in this workbook is how to move toward positivity by honoring yourself and others. It has been proven scientifically by a brilliant woman named Barbara Fredrickson that when people receive more positive emotion and build character strengths and virtues that we will call "inner wealth," they see more in terms of "we" instead of "me." This also opens our minds and hearts enabling us to be creative and come together to overcome obstacles. One of the most powerful outcomes that came out of her study is that race did not seem to matter to anyone—"we" meant we did not see ourselves separate from another race but more together as in "we" in a tribal sense.

Tribes have strong social interactions among themselves that include altruism or positive interactions with others who they may not know as well as those they do know. Altruism is an unselfish way of relating to others, meaning that the welfare of that other person is a priority. Tribal groups have a strong sense of unity and they identify with one another in a more interrelated or mutual manner. In other words, they care about each other and will go out of their way to take a stand for each other and for the things they believe in.

The important caveat or warning is that the *Tribal Warriors* we are creating are a 100% peaceful, non-violent tribe. However, this tribe is completely committed to taking a warrior stand against any kind of violence, hate crimes, oppression, teasing, sarcasm, self-destruction, etc. This tribe holds to the principles of the following three stands derived from the Nurtured Heart Approach®. In other words, this is what they fight for in warrior-like fashion:

Stand One:

Refuse to Energize Negativity ("Absolutely NO!")

Stand Two:

Relentlessly Energize the Positive ("Absolutely YES!")

Fiercely recognize what is going strong rather than what is going wrong.

Create success and positivity any chance you get.

Stand Three:

Clearly and Unenergetically Enforce Limits (Absolute Clarity)

Set up clear limits and stick to strict consequences when the rules are broken.

Maintain personal boundaries with a clear code of conduct.

By sticking together as a tribe we can extinguish negativity in our personal lives, with our friends, in our families and in our schools and communities. "United we stand, divided we fall" is a very popular motto used by many nations and states, and it has also been used in songs. Think about it in this way: unless people are united, it is easy to destroy them. When people come together to take a stand, a powerful force of unity is created. A warrior can be described as a person who is brave and courageous. A warrior has a strong intensity toward action and effects change. She is strong minded and cares for her body. He is well-balanced and keeps his mind and heart open to learning and changing but never forgets he is part of a tribe. A warrior is fierce, assertive and energetically ready to take a stand at any given moment.

> **"The warrior stance is not always fearless - but it SHOWS GREAT COURAGE IN THE FACE OF FEAR. It predetermines goals and shows focused intention in all circumstances. That is what makes it powerful."**
>
> —*Laura Montané-Bailey, LMFT Certified Nurtured Heart® Specialist*

Laura Montané-Bailey, Certified Nurtured Heart® Specialist, suggests this Tribal Warrior Chant:

"We are those who fight hatred, and devote ourselves to building inner wealth in ourselves and those around us. Our weapons are strength of purpose, undaunting perseverance, and peaceful power. We always carry the spirit of the Tribal Warrior."

Perhaps you poets or potential songwriters or rappers can create a Tribal Warrior Chant too. Send it to us on our blog: **tribalwarriorsblog.com**.

The goal is to build inner wealth within you and then to change the world by creating inner wealth billionaire relationships at home, in school and in communities.

TRIBAL WARRIORS:
Life Skills to Optimize Well-Being for Teens

SECTION ONE:

Building Personal Inner Wealth

Introduction

This book was created to fill a gap in what I noticed as a missing piece of the puzzle in all the workbooks and programs that are out there for teens. Many of them are amazing and wonderful tools that we have used over the years to teach teens how to feel better and stay better but like anything else, this field keeps growing and changing. We are thankful for the researchers who help us prove that! In addition, we have found that pre-teens and teenagers do not always want to complete an entire workbook on one subject. I have designed *Tribal Warriors* to be an Action Guide that pulls some of the most powerful ideas together in one place. You can decide to learn any concept at much deeper levels, and this guide will provide you with the basic tools to do so and will hopefully also spark your interest.

10 years ago I got turned on to positive psychology and I thought, WOW, this fits in so well with what I believe about helping people, adults and teens alike. I cannot tell you how many times I have heard, "I don't want to talk about it." We are trained in the field of psychology to engage people to talk things out, and honestly, that can be a very good thing. It is just not so great when it gets dragged on for too long or if you talk it out and then don't know what to do with those strong feelings. That is why when I chose things to get trained in, I chose things that would help people to get better as quickly as possible and would give them the tools to independently stay better. ***The ability to change our minds can be very effective. The power to believe in yourself and increase your well-being carries even more weight.***

Positive psychology enhanced this process thanks to a pretty smart guy named Dr. Martin Seligman who spoke about all of us in the field of psychology needing to focus on our strengths as well as the things that disturbed us. He also noted that we left millions of people and teens out—the ones who did not have a psychiatric disorder or a "label." We need to include everyone in this and assist each and every person to become **OPTIMIZED** in life. And when this happens, we all flourish. I don't know about you, but focusing on strengths and building you up from the inside out and using those strengths in activities that you like seem like pretty cool ways to either make you feel better, act better or achieve your goals.

What is exciting in the new research that has come out of this movement is that Martin Seligman and other brilliant researchers from around the world identified that positive psychology is not just about the science of happiness. Our well-being overall is really what matters. The new research almost a decade later tells us that positive emotion, engagement, positive relationship, meaning in life and accomplishment (PERMA) are

Introduction

the goals we should be working toward. I am completely on fire knowing this because I know how to get you and anyone else optimized in life if you are willing to learn.

Almost along the same time as the modern day positive psychology movement was forming, this creative and brilliant guy named Howard Glasser was developing a strategy to help parents work with very challenging, intense children in his work as a therapist. He noticed that teens and their parents had much more energy when they were locked into negative behavior like arguing or when things were going wrong. He realized intuitively, deep in his gut, that many things he had been taught as a therapist were not working very well, and this bothered him. For almost the last two decades he has worked tirelessly to bring the Nurtured Heart Approach® into the world. This is pretty exciting because it is now being used in many schools, homes, and workplaces, and its use is spreading all around the world. I feel pretty lucky to be a part of this social movement.

There is one thing I want you to notice throughout this workbook. I will be very clear about the different things that I am teaching you. There are some very powerful positive psychology activities as well as some techniques that will help you get things cleared up in your head that I learned and want to share with you. You will see that I will honor and recognize their creators, BUT I will be enhancing some of them with creative names that have Nurtured Heart® flair. I am not sure if you ever heard of a product called Miracle-Gro®. It helps plants and flowers grow bigger and stronger. The Nurtured Heart Approach® is like Miracle-Gro® in real life, and whether we use it alone or with something else, we see extraordinary things happen. So get ready to change your life!

And now, it is your turn to get infected with positivity. Let me start by telling you a bit about my fantasy school. Believe it or not, *some* schools are doing some of this already all around the United States and in other countries. It is my wish that every school would do *all* of this to get all teens optimized in life.

The Greatness Academy

Activity 1.1 — Activity 1.4

The Greatness Academy

There is something different about Greatness Academy. Teens flourish there. All teens… not just some teens—all teens. Upon entering the school, middle and high school aged preteens and teens are hustling to get to their classrooms. There is an energy of positivity that pulses though the hallways.

The principal is such a cool dude. His name is Howard Glasser. The teens call him "Dr. G" for greatness. He believes in the inherent greatness of all teens. In other words, you are born with greatness but sometimes you lose it along the way for one reason or another so he teaches us how to bring it back. He believes that if us grown-ups reflect your greatness to you that you will in turn stand in your greatness. Don't worry, you will be learning in more detail what greatness is and how you get it.

It gets even better. You all learn how to relate better to everyone in your life. Friends. Siblings. Teachers. Parents. You even learn how to get along with people who are different than you are, and bullying, teasing and sarcasm rarely happen at Greatness Academy. We will talk later about what happens when teens get off track.

You may not believe this but something happens to you that you cannot stop when you are treated in such a way. Something starts to grow and then flourish inside you. It's called "inner wealth" and it is a pretty cool thing to own.

Dr. G understands that enhancing your well-being in the school setting will not only make you a better student but more importantly will build you up from the inside out. Once

that happens, we see decreases in depression and drug and alcohol abuse, less conflict among students and even better relationships at home with parents. The key is you get built up from the inside out and the truth is at Greatness Academy, you are cared about more as a person rather than a student. The cool news however is that you end up doing your best in school and you are better equipped to achieve your goals as a student.

The Greatness Academy

Let me introduce you to some caterpillars and butterflies that help me show you how this is done. Yeah I know. Sounds a little weird, right? Just stay with me. And NO! You all don't have to dress like caterpillars and butterflies when you do this in your school. Come on now! ☺ But first I want to explain to you the "why" of using the concept of caterpillars and butterflies and how it relates to us human beings.

Why Caterpillars and Butterflies?

> "There is nothing in a caterpillar that tells us it's going to be a butterfly."
> —*Buckminster Fuller (1895–1983), inventor and architect*

Why caterpillars and butterflies? Caterpillars need to find the right stuff to eat in order to move through their childhood and teen years into young adult butterflies. If they do not get the right food, they won't make it or they will struggle to get there successfully. In this story the "right stuff" is the food the caterpillars eat that builds inner wealth or positivity. The "wrong stuff," or in other words negativity, is how they get off track.

Anyone who watches a caterpillar for any length of time knows that its main driving force in life is its appetite. It has an intense need to obtain as much nourishment as possible to prepare for transformation. Caterpillars eat constantly—and they can't eat just anything. Each breed of caterpillar needs a different kind of food, and in abundance, in order to change and grow into a magnificent butterfly.

If you think about how this can relate to people, think about how different and unique we all are and all the different traditions that human beings celebrate. We all eat different cultural meals and have special family habits around meals. And each child, regardless of what choices of food she or he eats, grows into a beautiful person like the caterpillar grows into a magnificent butterfly. And there are many spectacular butterflies of all colors, shapes and sizes, just as with us people. We come in many beautiful shapes, sizes and colors from all around the world and we learn at the Greatness Academy how to embrace those differences and how to respect and honor each other.

Similarly, we human beings require a huge amount of nutrition to grow and transform—but not the caloric kind (most of us get too much of that). We thrive most when we receive abundant *spiritual and psychological* nutrition in the form of love and positive relationship—just like the relationships cultivated between the Tribal Warriors and Isabella that you will be reading about very soon.

When we say love, we do not mean how you may feel about someone you like in a romantic way. That is cool too but not what we mean. It is love toward ourselves and others.

The Greatness Academy

Kindness and compassion. Caring. Our appetites for this kind of positive relationship exist just as much in families, in schools and in communities as they do in any other area of your life.

In preparation for metamorphosis, the caterpillar weaves a silken chrysalis—a word derived from the Greek word for gold. It demonstrates that while change is inevitable, it doesn't have to be painful. For us humans, positive relationship helps us to relax into transformation. It gives us the hope, faith, and sense of self-worth we require to keep morphing into greater and greater versions of ourselves. And this is what makes a school setting really golden: students who already see themselves as successful and who genuinely want to build further success.

Butterflies are regarded as symbols of peace, happiness, and fidelity. In various cultures, butterflies have been symbolic of resurrection, the soul, eternal life, young love, transition, lightness, and beauty. They have been called "flowers that fly." In central Asia, Aztec Mexico, New Zealand, and Zaire, as well as in Christian mythology, the butterfly is considered a symbol of the soul. In Greek mythology, psyche (the Greek word for "soul") is symbolized by a butterfly. Ancient Christian tombs often included a depiction of a butterfly. Christ has been illustrated holding a butterfly in many works of art.

The caterpillar unquestioningly enters into transformation. Her body and her environment change in shocking ways as she follows her destiny. As she goes into the dark night of metamorphosis to emerge completely transformed, she exemplifies trust and hope—a model of transformation for those who are held back from becoming their greatest selves by fear or uncertainty. The butterfly's transformation is a fitting symbol for the life journey of the human being. Hopefully, the twists, turns, setbacks, and successes we experience all contribute to morphing us into what symbolism writer Avia Venefica calls "ever-finer beings."

As our caterpillar-selves transform into butterfly-selves we realize that, contrary to what Buckminster Fuller said about caterpillars and butterflies, our butterfly-selves—our qualities of greatness—were in us all along. That butterfly-ness was in our DNA just as butterfly-ness is in the DNA of the caterpillar. The metamorphosis is just about changing the expression of what we have always possessed. And that is precisely what Dr. G believes. Our greatness is in us all along.

And so the story goes…

The Greatness Academy

Isabella and Justice

Isabella is in the tenth grade. She has attended Greatness Academy for three years. She is part of the Tribal Warriors because she has risen to be a leader at the school. It hasn't been an easy ride for her but she has managed to shine and to work through her problems. There were times when she was not ready to be a leader but with perseverance she remained on track.

She is flourishing and actually likes coming to school every day. She gets a lot of support with her school work and she is appreciated by all her teachers and school staff. Most importantly, the teens at this school support one another. They build each other up instead of tearing each other down. And if Isabella makes a mistake or takes a wrong turn, there is no drama. She is called out on it with what they call a "reset" and then she is back on track with a focus on what is going strong rather than what is going wrong.

At Greatness Academy they have a program where one student is partnered with another student. Sort of like a mentoring program. Isabella is partnered with Justice. She has her work cut out for her but she is equipped to handle it and ready for the challenge. She notices that Justice gets very stuck. Justice is really smart and can be very funny. Unfortunately he has not learned yet how to make the best choices and he is commonly eating a lot of junk of food in the form of negative self-talk. He allows himself to be plagued with worrying, misery and doubtfulness.

In all fairness to Justice he is dealing with a lot at home. Life can be difficult sometimes and it is not easy just because you are a teenager. The amazing thing about Justice though is that he has so many great things about him but he often cannot see them. Sometimes he just won't let anyone help and that is a big mistake. He gets off track a lot, and all the teachers, Dr. G and the Tribal Warriors are relentless in their pursuit to take him to his highest potential. You see, when we have inner wealth, we can deal with life and all its challenges. For real!

Isabella notices that Justice sneaks in junk food with lots of sugars, dyes and bad carbohydrates. She notices that right after he eats that junk it is like he is on drugs and then shortly after he crashes. He knows he is not supposed to eat that stuff. He has a label. ADHD, Attention Deficit Hyperactivity Disorder. His mom does not want him on medication and she works hard to feed him healthy food at home and encourages him to exercise and stay active. By the way, Greatness Academy has a different definition for ADHD. It is called our life force, or our intensity, and it is not something to medicate away but rather to channel into positivity.

The Greatness Academy

Greatness Academy has a rule about no junk food. In fact they use a program called Natural Ovens Bakery as a meal plan for breakfast and lunch. This change has made a huge difference in the school and other schools too like Appleton Central Alternative High School in Wisconsin. YO! I am serious. For real. Check it out yourself. Read "Students Behave Better with Healthy Lunch" from ABC News. I included the article for you to read later. Now let's get back to transforming Justice.

The Three Opponents: WMDs
(Worry, Misery & Doubt: Weapons of Mass Destruction)

Justice gets himself bogged down with negative thinking and not so smart choice making. On top of dealing with all his energy and trying to learn ways to focus with the help of his teachers, he pretty much battles three major opponents: Worrying William, Miserable Marvin and Doubting David. He has still yet to apply "reset" to himself to shake off this negativity but he is learning. All the staff at Greatness Academy and the student Tribal Warriors are working with him. Sometimes it gets on his last nerve while other times he responds to it and they see glimpses of change.

Worrying William worries about practically everything that ultimately leads him to a state of anxiety. When Justice fuels the thoughts that come from this part of his brain he starts his entire day worrying before he even gets out of bed in the morning. He has not learned to ask himself, "How is worrying about this or that going to help me? Is my worrying going to change anything? Will worrying solve my problems? Does worrying about failing a test help me pass it? How is worrying preventing me from studying? How is worrying affecting my stomach? Does worrying about mom and dad divorcing make it any different?" If Justice opened his mind to get help with this, he would learn how to counteract these irrational thoughts and his anxiety would be reduced if not eliminated.

Although it is healthy to be *concerned* about things in life, worrying leads to anxiety and sometimes lots of stressful toxins inside our bodies. We will talk more later about healthy and unhealthy negative emotions but this is one example.

Miserable Marvin is moody and for the most part in a state of depression. He refuses to talk to anyone about it or get help. He makes poor choices like sometimes using alcohol and smoking weed to feel better. He claims he is a social drug user but truth be told he is using drugs to change his mood. When he is in a really bad mood, he sometimes can be very mean to others around him. He may bully, tease or be sarcastic especially if he is feeling lonely or down on himself.

When Justice has gotten himself swallowed up in misery with Marvin, he can get in a lot of trouble. He even wonders to himself, "Why am I being this way?" or "Why am I doing these things?" But he just cannot seem to shake it. Justice is not proud of this but he did a lot of bullying and teasing in his old school and at times he falls back into that trap. He pretty much started bullying after he was bullied. He also realized that he got a lot of attention and made some friends when he picked on other teens and he became part of that group. He came to realize over time that those friends were all in trouble most of the time. Although he misses their "friendship" he eventually was able to see that hanging out with them was getting him into a lot of trouble. And like him, all those teens were good teens inside but for one reason or another they had bad behavior and attitude problems.

Justice has a right to be sad or angry just like anyone else. These are natural feelings. Sometimes he gets disappointed, which is another healthy negative emotion, but it quickly spirals into depression, which is unhealthy. When he gets angry for some reason he often flies into a rage and he gets out of control. Instead of talking about how he is feeling either with his Mom, friends or a school counselor, he often makes other self-destructive and impulsive choices.

When Justice lapses into the Doubting David side of his brain, this is the time when Justice is rating himself and others in a very negative way. He puts himself down and starts to believe he is not good enough. He begins to get off track with school and sometimes even isolates himself from his friends at school. The problems intensify at home with his mother because he stops doing his homework and refuses to follow the rules. He doubts himself and his ability in everything so much so that he begins to lose his luster as he shuts himself off from the world. And this is precisely why the Greatness Academy is the best place for him to be.

The Tribal Warriors

Isabella is a member of the Tribal Warriors. This team is comprised of five outstanding leaders who are responsible for creating new leaders as they move through high school. Of the five, two are Junior Leaders—one is a freshman, one a sophomore—and the other three are Senior Leaders in their junior and senior years. It is designed this way to sustain the program in the school. The Tribal Warriors are responsible for grooming and training the middle school teens. Membership is not mandatory but most teens want to join and they grow and change together.

The Tribal Warriors are comprised of Kool Kodak, Polaroid Power, Clarity Canon, Creative Chris and Raphael Reset. In any school year the gender can change for any leadership role. Clarity Canon, Creative Chris and Raphael Reset are always Senior Leaders because their responsibilities are a bit more sophisticated as they need to have

The Greatness Academy

leadership skills that embrace all the leadership techniques we are learning here, and they need to deliver their share with perseverance and precision in a more notched up way.

Kool Kodak is a pretty cool dude. He seems to notice everything that's going right. Whomever he speaks to comes away feeling special. Even if it's something small—a choice to follow the rules, or handling strong feelings, or just showing up and paying attention—he has something good to say about it. Practically everywhere he goes, Kool Kodak takes "snapshots" of successes, both miniscule and massive, and he's extremely generous when giving feedback to team members about those successes. Another way to think about Kool is to imagine that you hold a mirror up in front of someone and just describe what you see. You are not being fake, just making real observations. The "kool" news is that you can even apply this technique to someone that you do not know or maybe that you do not even like so much. You know those annoying students or maybe one of your brothers or sisters who gets on your last nerve. With this technique, it helps you communicate with others in a real way instead of ignoring or perhaps arguing with someone.

Polaroid Power comes in with a zoom lens and really lays it on thick. As a more seasoned student, she can keep up with Kool Kodak in terms of noticing and acknowledging success. Like a Polaroid camera, she captures success as it happens, then deepens that image of success by clearly stating how the success reveals strengths and virtues. Her unique, intense style takes some getting used to, but in the end this ability to hone in on what's going right—and on what's so right about it—makes her an invaluable leader of the team.

Clarity Canon is the team's ultimate school policy implementer and relentless rule follower, but she's not one to lecture, reprimand, or scold when rules are broken. Instead, she recognizes *rule-following*. She keeps students in full compliance by offering frequent reminders to those staying on task: *you are wonderful for not breaking rules and for following policy.* Clarity Canon appreciates fellow students for their willingness to change old habits, for staying in healthy control and for re-routing themselves back to compliance when they break rules or fail to comply with school policies and procedures. She's firm and strict, but also compassionate, loving, and proactive.

Creative Chris believes beyond reason that all students can flourish. His view is that giving recognition for every success, brilliance, and accomplishment is good for everyone, including the one who gives that recognition. He notices what his fellow students are doing in the moment—or even what they're wearing!—and takes the time to tell them what he's observing. He communicates to the other students that he values them for positive attitude and great work ethic. While he sometimes can sound like his other team leaders, there is something unique about him and his technique.

Even when students seem to be having a rough day, he finds ways to positively acknowledge them for their ability to deal with hard times or difficult tasks. The really interesting thing about Creative Chris is that he has this ability to notice even the slightest movement toward positive change and he is quick to jump on it. It is like he has superpowers for seeing these things. It's like he has a hawk eye for that detailed, minute movement and then he swoops in and notices it publicly!

Creative Chris is especially magnificent at bringing students back to balance when necessary. Indeed he is often the one who is able to de-escalate crises at the school and his team members elaborate on what he does. While he doesn't always hit the mark, he responds to his own errors and negative thoughts by redirecting his focus to what's great and right in the moment.

Raphael Reset is the one who helps us get right back on track. He believes that a rule broken is a rule broken. A little bit of hurting yourself or others is hurting yourself or others. If he sees anyone arguing, he comes right in and resets them back to their great qualities and restores peaceful communication. He is pretty cool because sometimes you do not even know you have been reset. His technique is very powerful because he teaches us about healing and feeling better quickly by staying on track and working to achieve any goal we set. Raphael Reset does not allow us to make things worse by feeding negative thoughts or behaviors for even a second!

The big trick with all of these ways to show radical appreciation is to eventually learn how to radically appreciate and recognize your own strengths. Focus on what is going strong rather than what is going wrong. Students who make it to these leadership roles are without question students who have awesome "inner wealth," and that is because they have managed to apply these techniques to themselves despite any of their backgrounds and labels, or any of the hard times they experienced in their childhood and teen years.

Let's take a look at a school day at Greatness Academy…

Monday Morning

Isabella arrives at school just on time. Like Justice she can at times default to some negative

Isabella, you are here just in time! You are definitely a shining role model for other students by following the rule of not being late.

Thanks, Clarity. I appreciate you saying that today because I was almost late but still managed to get here on time.

thinking but she has truly learned how to reset herself from doing that. This morning was one of those times. She was a little frustrated that she barely made it to school on time and she was a little tired today. Instead of focusing on her frustration, she decided to notice that she did make it to school on time and told herself that she was being responsible and it was okay that she was not early. She also noticed that in spite of her challenges to get up on time, she still managed to get herself organized and get out the door with enough time to make it to school just a few minutes before the bell rang.

As she was coming through the door she ran into Clarity Canon and what she said to Isabella sealed the deal. "Isabella, you are here just in time! You are definitely a shining role model for other students by following the rule of not being late." Isabella started to feel a little better just after hearing those words and replied, "Thanks, Clarity. I appreciate you saying that today because I was almost late but still managed to get here on time." Clarity acknowledged what Isabella said and shared with her what she does to avoid being late for school. She told her that it was not always easy for her either even though she always seemed to be early for everything. Clarity changed some bad habits and made some changes in her routine that help her with time management. This exchange really helped Isabella and she was glad that she opened up to Clarity about her challenge. It is nice to know that she is not the only one who struggles with getting to school on time, and it was even better to learn some tips to make it easier.

About five minutes after the bell rang, Justice comes slithering through the door hoping no one will notice him being late. As luck would have it, there was Dr. G. It figures. Dr. G is there without fail every morning to greet the students and he purposely waits for the

The Greatness Academy

stragglers. Dr. G doesn't ignore that they are late. There are always consequences for being late and everyone knows that. A rule broken is a rule broken. One minute late is one minute late. Justice already knows he will be doing his community service later. What Dr. G pays attention to is that they actually made it to school and that's even more important than being late.

Dr. G says hello to Justice and says, "Thanks for getting here, Justice. I know Mondays can be hard for everyone, even me." Justice says thanks but thinks to himself, "Yeah, even harder when you decide to stay out late with the wrong crew on a Sunday night and drink beer and smoke weed and your Mom refuses to call you out sick for school." Dr. G picks up right away on Justice's mood. "Justice, I see that you look a little angry or down. If you want to talk, let us know. Ms. Bravo is here today too. It must have been hard for you to get here today but I am glad you did."

Justice likes Ms. Bravo. She is the school's student assistance counselor. She is liked so much that teens seem to try and get into trouble just to spend time with her. But she is way too smart for that. In fact, she does not allow teens to randomly come to her office. What she does instead is work with the teachers to keep teens in the classrooms. She also runs morning, lunch and after school groups for teens who want to talk and she teaches them how to handle their strong feelings and manage their own negative behavior. At Greatness Academy, they believe that teens need to be "timed in," and it is valued when teens stay in their classes and learn.

Some teens, like Justice, are assigned to some of these groups. Ms. Bravo works with Mrs. Elsey, a resource teacher at the middle school who is the innovator of the Tribal Warriors. Together they coach and energize them to take their roles to greater heights. They all alternate attending the groups with Ms. Bravo. She makes a lot of sense and is so easy to talk to but for some reason Justice is not in the mood for her today. He knows that Dr. G won't let it rest and he will likely tell Ms. Bravo what he noticed about Justice's mood. They work very closely together so there is no

The Greatness Academy

doubt Justice will hear from her today. Justice slithers toward his homeroom with very low energy.

Upon entering, Justice's home room teacher Miss Saskia welcomes him into the classroom. She doesn't make a sarcastic comment like they did at his old school. The teachers at his old school would say something like "nice of you to join us" or "glad you could make it." He used to feel so embarrassed when they called him out on stuff like that in front of all the other students, and he often would have no motivation to attend his old school because of it. Just like Dr. G, Miss Saskia greets him and welcomes him into the room. A couple of the other teens started making comments about him being late and Miss Saskia swiftly reset them all. One of the boys was mumbling and did not reset himself right away but he eventually did and he got recognized for pulling himself together—looks like he was off to a bad start this Monday too. Justice took his seat and began to get his things ready for first period. Miss Saskia noticed how quickly he reset himself and told him in front of all the other students how impressed she was that he was making good choices and being so mature.

Isabella is in the same first period class as Justice. As they are waiting for the class to start, Isabella notices his mood and obvious low energy. "Justice, what's up with you today? You seem sort of down." Justice told her that he did not want to come to school today because he was tired. Isabella's antennae perked up when she heard this. She knows her friend Justice very well and she hadn't heard from him this weekend. That normally means trouble. She realized she would need to notch things up today and says, "But

The Greatness Academy

you know what Justice, you are here. You could have cut school and hung out all day with your old friends who cut too but you chose to come here instead. That says so much about you and how much you are changing. You are also proving to yourself that you want to do better in school than you have in the past." Justice did feel a little better after hearing what Isabella said. "She is a good friend and mentor to me," he thinks to himself. Isabella also suggested that they grab their lunch and instead of eating in the cafeteria, they would attend Ms. Bravo's lunch time energy group. Isabella is notching it up big time.

Speaking of notching it up, the school has a pretty neat system that really helps students when they get off track. Dr. G does not want any student falling through the cracks, and he and the rest of the staff care about how teens are really doing inside, not just what kind of grades they are producing. If a teacher or school staff notices a student seems off, the school has a **Notch It Up** alert that goes off to all the teachers who have that student in their classes. Miss Saskia put out an alert for Justice and another student too. The Warrior teachers and the Tribal Warriors are forewarned and more than forearmed to take on this battle to get these teens back on the track to success.

Some teachers were not on board with this at first and complained about how much work they have to do already. They asked why they would have to take extra time out of their schedule to notch things up. Dr. G quickly reset them and reminded them that at Greatness Academy notching things up is a part of their philosophy. Over time he was able to prove to them that approaching students in this way actually increased teaching time and decreased challenges in the classroom with emotionally and behaviorally challenged teens. He also noted that all teens need to flourish and attending only to challenging behavior means leaving out all the other teens who deserve an optimized experience.

What is "Inner Wealth"?

Howard Glasser coined this term in his development of the Nurtured Heart Approach®. He created a set of ideas and strategies for adults to recognize, appreciate and reflect to a child his or her positive choices. As a result, inner wealth is created. Glasser describes this further as a deep and lasting kind of self-esteem that is built on actual experiences of being held in esteem day after day. He also refers to this as qualities of greatness that you already possess.

But sometimes, the adults in our lives have not always helped us build inner wealth, and for some teens, they never ever got recognized for positivity. Some teens are quiet and remain under the radar and don't get noticed. Some teens get in loads of trouble either with the law, at home or at school, or with drugs and alcohol. Some teens get challenged by illness whether medical or something like depression or attention deficit disorder. Others come from a really rough home life and get bounced around from place to place or live in chaos their entire childhoods where they cannot see their own inner wealth.

The good news is that despite what your life is like, you can make smart choices and seek out a better way. Sometimes it may not feel like it is worth it but we all grow up. We can choose to have a different life and it can start now.

Although it is best when adults in your life help you build your inner wealth, this book is designed to help you notice it yourself, which is an added bonus if the adults in your life are already helping you. My guess is if you have your hands on this book, someone who cares about you gave it to you. People like that are there for you and ready to show you the way. You just need to let them. It is your choice.

Okay. I am getting there. So what does this mean to you? Well let's answer some questions that will help you see whether or not you have inner wealth. Be completely honest. There is no right or wrong answer. If we need to upgrade to a new system of inner wealth, that is precisely what we will be doing so get ready to install some new software.

Activity 1.1

Whether you feel like you do or do not at this moment, you do have inner wealth. Howard Glasser teaches us to teach you what is already inside of you. We do that in a very simple way. It is like we just hold a mirror up and we reflect the wonderful qualities we are already seeing in you in the moment. For example, if you are paying attention to the person explaining this to you or reading this yourself here is what we notice:

"I notice you are listening and paying attention." By listening and paying attention you are showing that you have respect for the person working with you. You are being cooperative and appear to be open to learning something new. This also shows that you are willing to change and help yourself feel better if you were feeling down or anxious, or you are taking yourself to higher levels of optimization, or BOTH!

"I notice you are reading and asking questions." By reading on your own you are showing great learning and reading abilities. By asking questions you are inquisitive and curious about how things work. You likely ask a lot of questions and that reveals an assertive person as well as an intelligent person. People who ask a lot of questions are often very smart!

Remember I told you about all those positive psychology researchers before who have helped us prove that building you up makes sense? Well now is the time to do a little activity. By answering these questions, you can see how researchers do this. Go to **www.authentichappiness.org** with an adult's permission. If you are under 18, an adult needs to create a username and password. Complete the VIA Signature Strength Survey for Children that was designed for youth ages eight through 18. There are 24 character strengths that have been identified in positive psychology research as being prevalent around the world and across cultures. When you complete this questionnaire, you identify what are called your five "Signature Strengths." Don't worry if you see a strength that you would like to have and it is not one of your top five. We can work on that! The interesting thing is that your signature strengths can change over time depending on what you are doing in your life or how you are thinking and feeling. The most important thing to remember is that these strengths are already inside you and some are just stronger than others at this time.

Write down your Top Five Signature Strengths here:

Signature Strength One: _____

Signature Strength Two: _____

Signature Strength Three: _____

Signature Strength Four: _____

The Greatness Academy

Signature Strength Five: _____

What are your thoughts about these strengths? Are you surprised by what was revealed?

Are you disappointed? Are there other strengths you would prefer to see? Write down your thoughts:

_____

_____

Later on you are going to learn how to build these strengths even more, and you will learn how to build new ones too!

Now, below I want you to write down an activity that you would like to do that would enhance each of your top five signature strengths. If you get stuck, don't worry. Answer what you can and then go to the person who showed you this workbook for help. The idea is if you do an activity that is in line with each of your signature strengths, you will achieve higher levels of satisfaction in your life and this will improve your well-being. In a more powerful way you begin to move toward being optimized and this neat thing called "flow" happens to you.

Signature Strength One Activity Idea: _____

_____

Signature Strength Two Activity Idea: _____

_____

Signature Strength Three Activity Idea: _____

_____

Signature Strength Four Activity Idea: _____

_____

Signature Strength Five Activity Idea: _____

_____

If there is a strength that is not one of your top five but YOU want it to be, write it down here and the activity you would like to do to develop it stronger:

_____

_____

There is no doubt that you have heard of self-esteem. In a way, you can think of self-esteem as inner wealth but it is a bit more than that. There is some controversy or disagreement in the mental health field about self-esteem.

Inner Wealth is greater than self-esteem, but we do know that teens or adults who are exposed to more positivity, or the building of inner wealth, have better self-esteem.

Once again, by taking the survey below with 100% honesty, this is how we can scientifically measure your self-esteem before we begin our work together and then after to see if the number has changed. We hope, of course, to increase your inner wealth and see your self-esteem scores rise. We want you to take this in the beginning and then again when you finish this program.

Rosenberg's Self-Esteem Scale

www.wwnorton.com/college/psych/psychsci/media/rosenberg.htm

1. **I feel that I'm a person of worth, at least on an equal plane with others.**

   ☐ Strongly Agree   ☐ Agree   ☐ Disagree   ☐ Strongly Disagree

2. **I feel that I have a number of good qualities.**

   ☐ Strongly Agree   ☐ Agree   ☐ Disagree   ☐ Strongly Disagree

3. **All in all, I am inclined to feel that I am a failure.****

   ☐ Strongly Agree   ☐ Agree   ☐ Disagree   ☐ Strongly Disagree

4. **I am able to do things as well as most other people.**

   ☐ Strongly Agree   ☐ Agree   ☐ Disagree   ☐ Strongly Disagree

5. **I feel I do not have much to be proud of.****

   ☐ Strongly Agree   ☐ Agree   ☐ Disagree   ☐ Strongly Disagree

6. **I take a positive attitude toward myself.**

   ☐ Strongly Agree   ☐ Agree   ☐ Disagree   ☐ Strongly Disagree

7. **On the whole, I am satisfied with myself.**

   ☐ Strongly Agree   ☐ Agree   ☐ Disagree   ☐ Strongly Disagree

8. **I wish I could have more respect for myself.****

   ☐ Strongly Agree   ☐ Agree   ☐ Disagree   ☐ Strongly Disagree

9. **I certainly feel useless at times.****

   ☐ Strongly Agree   ☐ Agree   ☐ Disagree   ☐ Strongly Disagree

10. **At times I think I am no good at all.****

    ☐ Strongly Agree   ☐ Agree   ☐ Disagree   ☐ Strongly Disagree

Scores are calculated as follows:

For items 1, 2, 4, 6, and 7:	**For items 3, 5, 8, 9, and 10 (which are reversed in valence):
Strongly Agree = 3	**Strongly Agree** = 0
Agree = 2	**Agree** = 1
Disagree = 1	**Disagree** = 2
Strongly Disagree = 0	**Strongly Disagree** = 3

The scale ranges from 0-30. Scores between 15 and 25 are within normal range; scores below 15 suggest low self-esteem.

Have the person working with you double check your score and write down your total

score: _____

Do you agree with this? Does it make sense to you?

Explain: _____

_____

Let's also have you fill out another survey that will take a bit more time. These statements are directly related to Dr. G's idea that "inner wealth is a growing and deepening sense" of the items listed below. A deepening sense means it gets stronger over time within your mind and heart. We will also do this before and after our work together to see how this changes for you.

The Inner Wealth Scale

1. **I believe in other people.**

   ☐ Very Much Like Me   ☐ Mostly Like Me   ☐ Somewhat Like Me

   ☐ A Little Like Me   ☐ Not At All Like Me

2. **I believe in the goodness of others.**

   ☐ Very Much Like Me   ☐ Mostly Like Me   ☐ Somewhat Like Me

   ☐ A Little Like Me   ☐ Not At All Like Me

3. **I have the ability to not just learn new things but to understand how powerful that knowledge is to my life.**

   ☐ Very Much Like Me   ☐ Mostly Like Me   ☐ Somewhat Like Me

   ☐ A Little Like Me   ☐ Not At All Like Me

4. **I do not put myself down for mistakes I made in the past.**

   ☐ Very Much Like Me   ☐ Mostly Like Me   ☐ Somewhat Like Me

   ☐ A Little Like Me   ☐ Not At All Like Me

5. **I am able to stay focused in the moment.**

   ☐ Very Much Like Me   ☐ Mostly Like Me   ☐ Somewhat Like Me

   ☐ A Little Like Me   ☐ Not At All Like Me

6. **I do not worry about what will happen in the future.**

   ☐ Very Much Like Me   ☐ Mostly Like Me   ☐ Somewhat Like Me

   ☐ A Little Like Me   ☐ Not At All Like Me

7. **I am optimistic/hopeful about my life.**

☐ Very Much Like Me ☐ Mostly Like Me ☐ Somewhat Like Me
☐ A Little Like Me ☐ Not At All Like Me

8. **I believe I am a lovable son/daughter.**

☐ Very Much Like Me ☐ Mostly Like Me ☐ Somewhat Like Me
☐ A Little Like Me ☐ Not At All Like Me

9. **I am a caring friend.**

☐ Very Much Like Me ☐ Mostly Like Me ☐ Somewhat Like Me
☐ A Little Like Me ☐ Not At All Like Me

10. **I have a lot to offer in my contributions at school.**

☐ Very Much Like Me ☐ Mostly Like Me ☐ Somewhat Like Me
☐ A Little Like Me ☐ Not At All Like Me

11. **I am willing to change to have a better life.**

☐ Very Much Like Me ☐ Mostly Like Me ☐ Somewhat Like Me
☐ A Little Like Me ☐ Not At All Like Me

12. **I get excited about going to school and doing activities.**

☐ Very Much Like Me ☐ Mostly Like Me ☐ Somewhat Like Me
☐ A Little Like Me ☐ Not At All Like Me

13. **I can be very intense or moody and can handle that well.**

☐ Very Much Like Me ☐ Mostly Like Me ☐ Somewhat Like Me
☐ A Little Like Me ☐ Not At All Like Me

14. **I can handle strong angry, sad, or anxious feelings without hurting myself or others.**

   ☐ Very Much Like Me ☐ Mostly Like Me ☐ Somewhat Like Me
   ☐ A Little Like Me ☐ Not At All Like Me

15. **I am able to have close friendships and open up to others.**

   ☐ Very Much Like Me ☐ Mostly Like Me ☐ Somewhat Like Me
   ☐ A Little Like Me ☐ Not At All Like Me

16. **I realize that even though things may not go the way I want them to I can find ways to be successful.**

   ☐ Very Much Like Me ☐ Mostly Like Me ☐ Somewhat Like Me
   ☐ A Little Like Me ☐ Not At All Like Me

17. **I respect my body and I care for it with good hygiene, eating healthy, and exercising.**

   ☐ Very Much Like Me ☐ Mostly Like Me ☐ Somewhat Like Me
   ☐ A Little Like Me ☐ Not At All Like Me

18. **I am curious about the world and want to learn more.**

   ☐ Very Much Like Me ☐ Mostly Like Me ☐ Somewhat Like Me
   ☐ A Little Like Me ☐ Not At All Like Me

19. **I trust people most of the time in my life and believe there are good people in the world.**

   ☐ Very Much Like Me ☐ Mostly Like Me ☐ Somewhat Like Me
   ☐ A Little Like Me ☐ Not At All Like Me

20. **I have a purpose in life.**

☐ Very Much Like Me ☐ Mostly Like Me ☐ Somewhat Like Me

☐ A Little Like Me ☐ Not At All Like Me

21. **I realize that I can achieve great things in my life when I realize that great things are often the regular things I do daily.**

☐ Very Much Like Me ☐ Mostly Like Me ☐ Somewhat Like Me

☐ A Little Like Me ☐ Not At All Like Me

22. **I enjoy a number of things in my life whether at home, school, or in my free time.**

☐ Very Much Like Me ☐ Mostly Like Me ☐ Somewhat Like Me

☐ A Little Like Me ☐ Not At All Like Me

23. **I can create an intention for a goal I want to achieve.**

☐ Very Much Like Me ☐ Mostly Like Me ☐ Somewhat Like Me

☐ A Little Like Me ☐ Not At All Like Me

24. **I accept myself without conditions or judging myself. I can love myself.**

☐ Very Much Like Me ☐ Mostly Like Me ☐ Somewhat Like Me

☐ A Little Like Me ☐ Not At All Like Me

25. **I accept others without conditions or judgment. I accept them for who they are.**

☐ Very Much Like Me ☐ Mostly Like Me ☐ Somewhat Like Me

☐ A Little Like Me ☐ Not At All Like Me

26. **I like my life.**

☐ Very Much Like Me ☐ Mostly Like Me ☐ Somewhat Like Me

☐ A Little Like Me ☐ Not At All Like Me

27. **I realize there are truths and lies in this world. I am drawn to the truth more than I am to lies.**

☐ Very Much Like Me ☐ Mostly Like Me ☐ Somewhat Like Me

☐ A Little Like Me ☐ Not At All Like Me

28. **I am able to make good decisions by listening to what I know is the difference between right and wrong in my mind.**

☐ Very Much Like Me ☐ Mostly Like Me ☐ Somewhat Like Me

☐ A Little Like Me ☐ Not At All Like Me

29. **I have the power to be in healthy control of my thoughts and my actions and can accept people on a heart or soul level for who they are.**

☐ Very Much Like Me ☐ Mostly Like Me ☐ Somewhat Like Me

☐ A Little Like Me ☐ Not At All Like Me

30. **I know that sometimes it is okay to let things go for a better outcome. I do not have to win all the time or argue everything.**

☐ Very Much Like Me ☐ Mostly Like Me ☐ Somewhat Like Me

☐ A Little Like Me ☐ Not At All Like Me

31. **I can adapt to any situation even though I might get nervous about it or am afraid to change.**

☐ Very Much Like Me ☐ Mostly Like Me ☐ Somewhat Like Me

☐ A Little Like Me ☐ Not At All Like Me

32. **I can be happy without having to take risks that are unsafe.**

☐ Very Much Like Me ☐ Mostly Like Me ☐ Somewhat Like Me

☐ A Little Like Me ☐ Not At All Like Me

33. **I care about the environment and life on this planet.**

☐ Very Much Like Me ☐ Mostly Like Me ☐ Somewhat Like Me

☐ A Little Like Me ☐ Not At All Like Me

34. **I notice beauty in the world around me in things like nature, art, people, etc.**

☐ Very Much Like Me ☐ Mostly Like Me ☐ Somewhat Like Me

☐ A Little Like Me ☐ Not At All Like Me

35. **I do not want to end up with an addiction problem to drugs, alcohol, cigarettes, food, or unhealthy relationships.**

☐ Very Much Like Me ☐ Mostly Like Me ☐ Somewhat Like Me

☐ A Little Like Me ☐ Not At All Like Me

36. **I am supportive and kind to others.**

☐ Very Much Like Me ☐ Mostly Like Me ☐ Somewhat Like Me

☐ A Little Like Me ☐ Not At All Like Me

37. **I take responsibility for my actions or mistakes I make.**

☐ Very Much Like Me ☐ Mostly Like Me ☐ Somewhat Like Me

☐ A Little Like Me ☐ Not At All Like Me

38. **I can notice when other people are thoughtful and considerate.**

☐ Very Much Like Me ☐ Mostly Like Me ☐ Somewhat Like Me

☐ A Little Like Me ☐ Not At All Like Me

39. **I am a forgiving person.**

☐ Very Much Like Me ☐ Mostly Like Me ☐ Somewhat Like Me

☐ A Little Like Me ☐ Not At All Like Me

40. **I am thankful and appreciative of others actions directed at me.**

☐ Very Much Like Me ☐ Mostly Like Me ☐ Somewhat Like Me

☐ A Little Like Me ☐ Not At All Like Me

41. **I am an honorable person. I do the right thing and make good choices.**

☐ Very Much Like Me ☐ Mostly Like Me ☐ Somewhat Like Me

☐ A Little Like Me ☐ Not At All Like Me

42. **My family and friends can count on me to stick to my word. I am reliable.**

☐ Very Much Like Me ☐ Mostly Like Me ☐ Somewhat Like Me

☐ A Little Like Me ☐ Not At All Like Me

43. I have good judgment and make smart decisions.

☐ Very Much Like Me ☐ Mostly Like Me ☐ Somewhat Like Me

☐ A Little Like Me ☐ Not At All Like Me

44. **I am in general a respectful person.**

☐ Very Much Like Me ☐ Mostly Like Me ☐ Somewhat Like Me

☐ A Little Like Me ☐ Not At All Like Me

45. **I have a strong sense of respect and honor for many things in my life.**

☐ Very Much Like Me ☐ Mostly Like Me ☐ Somewhat Like Me

☐ A Little Like Me ☐ Not At All Like Me

46. **I understand the concept of loving and respecting others in the world.**

☐ Very Much Like Me ☐ Mostly Like Me ☐ Somewhat Like Me

☐ A Little Like Me ☐ Not At All Like Me

47. **I do love and respect others.**

☐ Very Much Like Me ☐ Mostly Like Me ☐ Somewhat Like Me

☐ A Little Like Me ☐ Not At All Like Me

48. **I believe I am capable of great things and can reach my goals.**

☐ Very Much Like Me ☐ Mostly Like Me ☐ Somewhat Like Me

☐ A Little Like Me ☐ Not At All Like Me

49. **I know that greatness can be found in the ordinary things in life.**

☐ Very Much Like Me ☐ Mostly Like Me ☐ Somewhat Like Me

☐ A Little Like Me ☐ Not At All Like Me

50. **Greatness is something I believe in for myself. I know I can achieve it.**

☐ Very Much Like Me ☐ Mostly Like Me ☐ Somewhat Like Me

☐ A Little Like Me ☐ Not At All Like Me

250–200:	You Are Flourishing and Have an Abundance of Inner Wealth
199–150:	Your Inner Wealth is Soaring to Greater Heights
149–100:	You Have Excellent Inner Wealth
99–50:	Great Inner Wealth
49–01:	Good Inner Wealth - You are Building Your Foundation

Inner Wealth Foundations

As you can see there is no such thing as not having Inner Wealth no matter how down, angry or frustrated you might sometimes feel. Even in your most challenging moments, you still have Inner Wealth. You still have character strengths and virtues. When we are working on improving ourselves at home, in school or with our friends, we can build on those foundations. Keep in mind that having Inner Wealth does not always mean that you are feeling positive or are in a good mood. You are being great when you are dealing with your moody self, or angry self, or sad self. But some days we all feel better than other days and sometimes certain things make us feel better or worse than others. Because you possess Inner Wealth, it is there for you to rely on especially in hard or challenging times.

The Pyramid of Inner Wealth

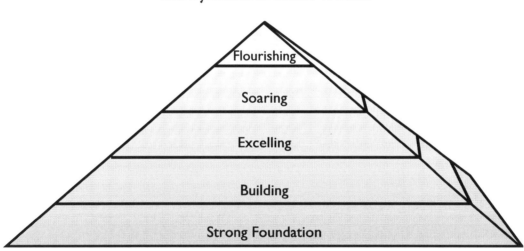

You may remember studying about the famous pyramids in Egypt that are part of ancient history. Take a look at the bottom portion of the above pyramid. It is the widest part of the pyramid and it supports the entire pyramid.

If you completed the above inner wealth survey and are disappointed because you scored low, well think again. Just like building a house or a pyramid, we need a strong structure to build on and that is just what you have. We need the foundation to keep building. We then work on excelling, soaring and ultimately flourishing.

The truth is that sometimes during life and all its challenges, no matter whether you are a teenager or an adult, we sometimes have to go back to our roots or our foundation and keep building from there. Life has many ups and downs as I am sure you already know. Just like we are getting back to our roots to work together in a tribe, we also need to be sure we have a strong foundation.

Activity 1.2

intellectual resources	physical resources
develop problem-solving skills	develop coordination
learn new information	develop strength and cardiovascular health

social resources	psychological resources
solidify bonds	develop resilience and optimism
make new bonds	develop sense of identity and goal orientation

By working on building your Inner Wealth, something else pretty cool is happening inside you. Your entire body is shifting. Every cell in your body is changing and storing Inner Wealth and positivity. Psychologically, in your mind a *broaden and build effect* is happening (Fredrickson, B). The more positive emotions that we experience help us to outweigh the unhealthy negative emotions that can drag us down by creating self-defeating behaviors, such as hurting ourselves or others either emotionally, verbally or physically. By increasing positivity, we are building our Inner Wealth and we become more resilient.

The Broaden and Build Theory of Positive Emotions explains how positive emotions are important to our survival. Positive emotions expand our thought and behavioral patterns and create a range of actions that our bodies and minds are ready to take. This creates flexibility with our thoughts or cognitions that result in resource building that is helpful to us over time. I am sure you have noticed that our emotions change quickly over time. There is a bonus in that the lasting effects are in the form of traits, social bonding and abilities that stay with us in the future. Fredrickson's work has shown us that positive emotions have tremendous value to human growth and development, and building more positive emotions helps us to lead fuller and more satisfying lives.

Google the word "resilient." Write down your findings here:

_____

_____

Google the word "resilient." Write down your findings here:

_____

_____

> "Greatness is the splendor of living one's dreams, the bounty of living one's passion and the valor of bringing that greatness to the world."
> —*Howard Glasser*

To practice greatness we work on *accusing* ourselves and others of the goodness we see even if it is the tiniest bit of goodness. What is something good you can see about yourself right now in this moment?

_____

_____

Write this down or type it in your Tribal Warrior Journal. Decide whether you want to use an electronic journal or handwritten journal. You are going to work on focusing on this good quality about yourself. You will grow this into greatness by giving it energy and recognition every single time you see it in you. Also practice noting this quality in others. For example, if you noticed that you are working hard right now on learning something new, notice when others are doing it too and tell them what you see.

Keep in mind that all this change is not easy and like anything else, it does take practice and hard work. Once you begin to experience your greatness and others' greatness, there is no turning back.

> "Once you commit fully to this warrior path of your own truth and that of others—greatness—then you are truly choosing the life your higher-self desires and envisions."
> —*Howard Glasser*

Googling Greatness Activity

This is an activity created by Howard Glasser in his book for adults, *You Are Oprah: Igniting the Fires of Greatness.* To prepare for this activity, go to google.com and search for something that interests you.

Write down how many results you get for that search here: _____

Let's imagine this. Go to **google.com** to see what happens when you Google your name with a + sign and the word greatness. For example, "Toni Anne Lofrano + greatness"

The Greatness Academy

What would you like to find in a Google search about you and your greatness?

_____

_____

Who are you in this moment? What qualities and strengths are you showing now?

_____

_____

What qualities and strengths would you like to own and practice building upon?

_____

_____

_____

What kinds of things are you interested in?

_____

_____

_____

This is you Googling your greatness. Take a moment to think about this but more importantly, take some long and complete breaths and take these thoughts or intentions into your heart. Notice you absorbing these qualities.

The Practice of Greatness

Dr. G says greatness comes from within; it's a state of being. It is something we are born with but sometimes we forget where it is. **Imagine this eight-point list as an upward spiral.**

Greatness is an Energy

**"The Greatness Practice is not about changing;
it's about choosing. Greatness is in our small choices."**

—Howard Glasser

---

1. **Accept It:** You are born with greatness and this is truth. When you try to deny this truth, you lose power to express your greatness. It takes a lot of energy to hide from the truth.

2. **See It:** Train yourself in the art of answering this question, "What's going right here?" Choose to see the things that are going right--things you think, say and do. Choose to see the things that aren't going wrong that could be going wrong. It requires practice.

3. **Think It:** Choose to focus on and to consider everything that's right that you are training your new eyes to see. Rather than thinking about your faults or things you do not like, focus on the things that are going well and things you have the power to change. That's using your power to expand and ignite your greatness.

4. **Appreciate It:** Choose to be grateful for the greatness and goodness that you are now able to see. Express your thankfulness. There are always deeper levels of gratefulness to explore.

5. **Feel It:** Emotions are so powerful that they sometimes scare us so we try to stuff or deny them. But feelings come from our hearts, and our hearts are the vehicles for transmitting greatness. The lie is that we have to act on our feelings. The truth is that we need only to feel them. Feel them with every cell of your body, and you'll be tapping into your life force.

6. **Do It:** When you accept your greatness and practice seeing it, thinking it and feeling it, there's no stopping you from creating greatness in your actions. You're the force of unstoppable greatness at home, at school and in your relationships.

7. **Be It:** By consistently choosing the Greatness Practice, it eventually becomes you. You're no longer concerned about "doing it" or "doing it right." You simply are. It is an internal state of being in complete alignment of spirit, soul and body.

8. **Live It:** The final stage is self-transformation and co-creation. Your soul gets to fulfill itself and bring your greatness to the world as a manifestation of who you really are.

Now it is time to develop a greatness routine. It is not reasonable to think that just because you complete every page of this workbook that it is the end of your journey. Growing and changing is a lifelong process as you move through each phase of your life. I have to be 100% honest with you. It is not easy to stay on a path of being disciplined, studying all the time as recommended, being respectful, following rules or making smart choices. It takes practice and commitment and more practice and more commitment.

It is easy to do the following activity with the tools that you will be learning. For now, I want you to start doing this activity at this point in the workbook to get into the practice of it. Down the road you will be learning more tools that will deepen this activity.

You may recall in the beginning of this workbook I mentioned Dr. Martin Seligman and positive psychology. He created an activity called "Three Blessings" or "What-Went-Well" activity. For the purposes of being creative and making this a Nurtured Heart Approach® activity, we are going to call this "TGT" or Three Greatness Things Daily Activity.

Practice Practice Practice

Whatever you decided about a journal, be sure that you are going to stick to it. We will be adding things on for you to notice as our work together continue. This needs to become part of your nighttime ritual. For best results, do this right before you go to sleep at night. Don't worry about this being right or wrong. For the most part you are going to notice what is going strong or going well. Remember later on we will show you how to add to this. As an FYI, this is an activity of Actively Recognizing YOU.

Let's practice. In this moment, what three things do you notice about yourself that are positive or are strengths of yours? For example, you are reading this chapter.

1. _____

2. _____

3. _____

Activity 1.4

If you are working with a group or a professional, share your statements or recognitions. Say them out loud. In doing so, not only are you helping yourself to anchor these TGTs into your brain and heart, you are helping someone else too. It's a WIN-WIN.

Here are some more examples:

- "I went to school today."

- "I did my homework today."

- "My friend was having a bad day and I spent some time listening to her."

You see from above that we are noticing the ordinary to make it extraordinary, as Dr. G from the Greatness Academy would say.

What is Your Energy?

Activity 2.1 — Activity 2.2

What is Your Energy

Over time I realized that no matter where I was or no matter who I worked with, I could feel an "energy" or a vibe from a person or a situation. I did not realize that, for a number of years, I thought of it somewhat like a pulse of a heart rate. I wrote a book several years ago and I gave it this title: *The Positivity Pulse: Transforming Your Workplace*. I wrote it for bosses and employers to learn how to get the "positivity pulse" in their workplaces. As I keep learning in my work and as a person, I have realized that I have to have a healthy and steady pulse within me in order to make change in my life, with others or in people's workplaces. I also realized that I needed to apply the things I learned to help others and myself. In order for me to stand in my own positivity, I needed to develop and nurture the greatness or positivity within me.

Let's look at different heart rates and the "pulse" that can be shown on one of those monitoring screens I am sure you have seen either at a hospital or on a TV show. It is very important for you to get in tune with your body and how it is feeling on many levels. We will talk later about nutrition and physical activity and how those things affect you too. For now we are going to pay attention to your "inner pulse" in the form of energy—positivity and negativity. You will notice when you are flourishing and how you can build on that. At the same time, you will learn how you can "reset" yourself away from your negativity and move toward success.

Healthy Pulse: When you have a healthy pulse everything is functioning properly. You are calm, in charge of your strong feelings and doing well in many aspects of your life. You are able to work through conflicts in a mature manner. You have positive friends, you are doing your best at school and you have some good relationships whether with an adult in your family, a friend or a professional in your life. You also are taking care of your physical self by making healthy choices with food and finding time for physical activity.

Stressed and Crazed Pulse: A stressed or crazed pulse means you are likely spiraling out of control. You feel very nervous or anxious, and you often make mistakes with the choices you make. In these times you may decide to abuse drugs and alcohol, not eat right or perhaps be angry and irritable with everyone you know. It may be hard to focus or concentrate when you feel so anxious, crazed or stressed.

Low Energy and Depressed Pulse: Hopelessness and depression may overwhelm you when your pulse drops this low. You may even feel like it is flat lining and you are void of feeling or experiencing joy. You refuse to allow others to help you and you refuse to help yourself. You may abuse alcohol or drugs in this phase, over-eat or refuse to eat, and may even refuse to shower and care for your hygiene. In severe cases, you could feel hopeless, you may not feel like being around anyone or you may even feel like hurting yourself.

Now you are going to be learning how to pay attention to, notice and recognize your "inner pulse."

How would you describe your personal inner pulse at this moment based on the examples above?

_____

_____

How would you describe the pulse or energy in your family?

_____

_____

Do you notice a difference in the pulse or energy in your family members? Is everyone the same?

What do you notice?

_____

_____

_____

How would you describe the pulse or energy at your school?

_____

_____

I want you to start really noticing your energy or your pulse in all areas of your life, and together we are building you up as a **Positivity Pulse Powerhouse**.

Activity 2.2

> "The ability to be in the present moment
> is a major component of mental wellness."
>
> —*Abraham Maslow*

> "If you have one eye on yesterday and one eye
> on tomorrow, you're going to be cockeyed today."
>
> —*Abraham Maslow*

Since the 1970s the world of psychology began to adopt the concept of staying in the present known as mindfulness. Basically it is the practice of staying in the moment. You bring your full attention to the present on a moment-to-moment basis. You do not hold on to yesterday even if yesterday was the greatest day of your life, and you do not focus on tomorrow. Stay in the moment. Focus on the moment.

Dr. G teaches us a new concept of mindfulness: Be here k**NOW**ing. Stay in the NOW knowing how you want to use your internal power. In the next section you are going to learn about intention, and staying in the NOW will assist you with the goals you have in your life.

Google "mindfulness quotes" and list three quotes below that make sense to you. Write each one on an index card. Keep them in a place where you can read them.

1. _____

2. _____

3. _____

Positivity and Rational Thinking is Healthy Thinking

Activity 3.1 — Activity 3.5

Positivity & Rational

What are labels? What kinds of labels am I referring to? For those of you who officially have a psychiatric diagnosis, for example, of depression, attention deficit hyperactivity disorder (ADHD), anxiety, oppositional defiant disorder, or conduct disorder to name a handful, I know YOU know what this means. I also know that you may have already received what we call a "laundry list" of labels depending on how you were behaving or what we call in the mental health field "presenting" at the time.

For those of you who do not have a "label" or psychiatric disorder, we need you to participate in this as well to help us break down the stigmatisms about mental health and learn to be more accepting and understanding of a person who does in fact have this challenge. Let's clear the air right at this moment and understand this statement: There is nothing "crazy" about having a psychiatric disorder. In fact with today's science and technology we know that people with ADHD, trauma, depression, anxiety or many other labels have clear changes in their brains that are different from people who do not experience these things. It is exactly like having a medical condition. In some instances, it is like having a cold or flu that may go away over time or that can be successfully managed with the right care.

For example, there is something we call adjustment disorder and this means exactly that. It means that something major may have happened in our lives and we are struggling with dealing with it. Sometimes we can get anxious or depressed or act out aggressively towards others because of that major life stressor even though it may have been through no fault or responsibility of our own. There is something else called bereavement and this means deep feelings of loss and grief that we can experience if we lost someone to a death or know we are losing someone to a terminal illness like cancer. Over time a person who is grieving or moving through the stages of loss can be anxious, angry or depressed.

Then there are other psychiatric disorders that will not go away such as a medical disorder like diabetes for example. But like diabetes, with the right support and interventions, we can get the symptoms in remission. This means we can lead healthy and productive lives with the right kind of help. Sadly there are times when depression and suicide can take adults or teens away from us. Sometimes people with psychotic features can also take their own lives. Many times adults and teens are hesitant to talk to others and feel very ashamed about having depression, anxiety, and ADHD to name a few of these diagnoses, or "labels."

We need to take a stand against thinking that there is something "crazy" or wrong with someone with a psychiatric label. We will talk later about other labels that are cruel and related to hate crimes.

In this activity you are just going to write down what you notice. There is no right or wrong answer, and your answer is private and confidential. It is best to be 100% honest while doing this. That is not always easy but you can be and are being a very honest person if you have gotten this far into this workbook. Everyone has great thoughts and feelings and everyone gets thoughts and feelings that are dark and not so attractive. At this point, I would like you to think about what you are thinking as it relates to yourself as someone with a psychiatric label. How are you treating yourself because of this label? Are you angry about it? Are you ashamed or embarrassed by it? Write down your thoughts here:

_____

_____

If you are not someone with a psychiatric label, think about what these labels mean to you.

Are you accepting of other students at school who have these labels? _____

Do you judge them because they may appear sad or withdrawn? _____

Do you do anything to make friends with or even just say hello to them? _____

Do you notice someone who seems angry all the time and has a tendency to get in trouble?

_____

Do you notice someone who seems to be bouncing off the walls and who has high energy?

_____

Do you judge these students or accept them for who they are? _____

Write down your thoughts here:

_____

_____

_____

Positivity & Rational

Positive Psychology Activity: Kindness

There is an activity that Dr. Seligman encourages and I would like to share it here with you. Find a kind thing to do for someone and just do it! ***Think of the Nike slogan: Just do it!*** Then notice what happens to you and your mood. Notice what happens in your heart energy. Write or type about this experience in your journal. Keep on being kind. It is really good for you and for others. Find someone or an organization that needs your help and volunteer. In New Jersey you can use **jerseycares.org** to find volunteer opportunities. Even if you are not in New Jersey, there are plenty of volunteer activities you can do as an act of kindness. Honestly, you can start right at home, at school or in your own neighborhood.

Tell your kindness story. Write down what you did here or post on **tribalwarriorsblog. com**:

_____

_____

_____

Did you help someone or something? If yes, describe who, what, when and how:

_____

_____

How did you feel about doing something kind for someone or some cause?

_____

_____

_____

Did you receive any feedback about what the others involved were feeling about what you did?

_____

_____

_____

What benefit did this have?

_____

_____

_____

NOTCH IT UP the Nurtured Heart® Way: Write down words that describe what you did and what values and strengths you showed by doing this act of kindness. This is you noticing yourself and recognizing your strengths and values.

_____

_____

_____

Positivity & Rational

Positive psychology is not new and did not just begin in your lifetime, your parents' lifetimes or even your great great great grandparents' lifetimes. Going back to ancient civilizations with known philosophers such as Socrates, Plato and Aristotle, human beings have been thinking about and trying to find answers about the "good life" for thousands of years.

Today's positive psychology research has been around for decades—close to 60 years. In the late 1990s, however, Dr. Martin Seligman became the architect for pulling together some brilliant thinkers from all around the world to get us to shift toward paying as much attention to what is going strong and not just what is going wrong in the field of psychology. We are taught that it is equally important to focus on our strengths as well as the behaviors, moods and thoughts that create challenges in our lives. He also said by only focusing on our weaknesses, we are leaving out a HUGE portion of the population… like 75–80% of people who do not ever have a psychiatric disorder or mental illness.

The most recent research reveals that human beings are most satisfied in life when they have more positive emotion, engagement, positive relationships, meaning and accomplishment (PERMA). When we have more of these things we are better off, healthier, more content and flourishing in life. The exciting news is that in our work together you are learning how to get more PERMA in your life using the Nurtured Heart Approach® either alone or as "Miracle-Grow" with other things.

P: Positive Emotion. Write down positive emotions that you are either feeling right now in this moment, have experienced in the past, or know about in general:

_____

_____

Positive emotion is the first building block of your well-being or a pleasant life. The pinnacle or highest positive emotion is love, but not love in the romantic way. More to come on this later.

E: Engagement. What does this mean to you? What does it feel like when you are doing something you really enjoy or love doing?

_____

_____

Think about a time when time stood still or when you were so completely involved in an activity that nothing else mattered. You may not have noticed that you were hungry or tired, and you may have been unaware of anything around you. Tell us about this time:

_____

_____

_____

NOTE: Remember "engagement" when we talk later about being in a state of flow.

R: Positive Relationship(s). What thoughts and feelings come to mind when you read the words "positive relationship?"

_____

_____

Being around other positive people creates a healthy support system for you. It also creates change within your cells when you build each other up and have strong, healthy relationships. Being kind and helping another person is good for both of you. Be selfish with kindness…spread it all around.

Who around you is a positive person? _____

What makes this person positive? _____

Remember this person (or people) for an activity later on called "An Attitude of Gratitude."

Write down one idea to take action toward kindness: _____

_____

Check out **randomactsofkindness.org** and be sure to post your idea on

tribalwarriorsblog.com

M: Meaning and Purpose. Write down something that has meaning to you or something you do that has a greater purpose other than for yourself:

_____

_____

Dr. Seligman describes meaning as "belonging to and serving something that you believe is bigger than the self" (Seligman, 2011). It is bigger than you. For example, you volunteer for a good cause like standing up against bullying and harassment of others. You do it because you believe in it. Your work and strong stance is for the greater good of your school and community and not because you want someone to notice you or because you have to do community service.

Positivity & Rational

A: Accomplishment or The Achieving Life: What does this mean to you? How do you feel when you accomplish something?

_____

_____

Accomplishment or achievement is about completing the goals we set for ourselves or that we choose to do for no other reason than because we want to.

Nurtured Heart® Greatness Practice: Stop now and notice yourself. What do you notice in this moment just by answering the above statements? Go ahead and notice TGT (Three Greatness Things). Create a sentence as if you were describing it to a blind person or as if you took a picture of yourself. For example, "I am participating and really thinking about how this applies to my life" or "I seemed to know right away what to write" or "I notice that even though I did not want to come to group today, I showed up and am learning something new."

1. _____

2. _____

3. _____

Now let's notch that up. We are going to add some values and character strengths to the three statements above. For each statement above, answer the question, "What does this show about me?" or "What value or strength am I showing?" For example, "I notice I completed this activity. That shows my ability to focus and concentrate." Add on the value or strength that you notice for the above three statements:

_____

_____

_____

_____

NEWS FLASH: Is this really good for you?

The Mayo Clinic, an extremely well-respected organization, states that positive thinking is linked to a wide range of health benefits including:

- Longer life span

- Less stress

- Lower rates of depression

- Increased resistance to the common cold

- Better stress management and coping skills

- Lower risk of cardiovascular disease-related death

- Increased physical well-being

- Better psychological health

You can see that it makes good sense to think positively and even more sense to notch it up to Greatness Thinking!

Positivity & Rational

> "So I like what I see when I'm looking at me
> When I'm walking past the mirror
> No stress through the night, at a time in my life
> Ain't worried about if you feel it
> Got my head on straight, I got my mind right
> I ain't gonna let you kill it"
>
> —*Mary J. Blige*

> "U.S.A. or Unconditional Self-Acceptance means that you can accept yourself 100% even when faced with failure or rejection by others. U.S.A. is a very healthy state to be in."
>
> —*Albert Ellis*

Do you accept yourself unconditionally? Albert Ellis, considered one of the great psychologists of our time, believed that we needed to love ourselves unconditionally.

Google or look up "unconditional" and write down what you find here:

_____

_____

When you accept yourself unconditionally, you are accepting yourself for who you are and you are not judging yourself. You accept yourself as a person who can and will make mistakes but you understand that those mistakes do not make you who you are. This does not mean you aren't going to feel self-conscious sometimes, especially as a teenager when you wake up with a big zit or acne all over your face. But it does mean that you will still accept yourself as a person who has acne.

> "In loving yourself unconditionally you will continue to have a strong sense of being there for yourself despite the acne. The acne isn't YOU. The greatness of your heart is the real you."
>
> —*Howard Glasser*

Write down something that you know you judge or criticize yourself for:

_____

_____

How can you accept this about yourself without judging yourself or putting yourself down?

_____

_____

What can you tell yourself instead? For example, "I have acne breakouts and even though I wish I did not have acne, it is part of life and I can live with it. I do not like it, but I can deal with it." Write your idea down:

_____

_____

Notch this up Nurtured Heart® Style and recognize how you are working to overcome negative thoughts about yourself. You are working on a plan to stop rating yourself and to start accepting yourself unconditionally without judging or criticizing yourself. What is your new statement?

_____

_____

TAKE ACTION: Do something about your acne or whatever the issue is! Talk to your parent(s) or school nurse and ask how you can take better care of your skin to reduce the amount of breakouts you have as well as to reduce how severe they get when you do not cleanse your face thoroughly.

KEY POINTS

Unconditional Self-Acceptance:

1. **I am a human being who makes mistakes. I have my good points and my bad points.**
2. **There is no reason why I must not have flaws.**
3. **Despite my good points and my bad points, I am no more worthy and no less worthy than any other human being.**

Positivity & Rational

Think about this. Write down the three strengths or things you like about yourself you believe you have right now in this moment:

1. _____

2. _____

3. _____

Ask someone close to you (a friend, a parent, a teacher) to name three things that they think is great about you:

1. _____

2. _____

3. _____

Even if you do not agree with them or if you struggled with writing down three of your own, ask yourself this: Can I accept myself unconditionally as a person who has all these qualities? If the answer is yes, in what ways do you think you can make them even stronger?

_____

_____

If you said no, ask yourself what is holding you back from accepting the greatness and strengths within you?

_____

_____

Consider taking one of the strengths that you feel unsure about. Just think about it. Don't force it. Don't push it. Just allow yourself to think about why you or someone else named that strength. What thoughts do you have?

_____

_____

Ask yourself if you deserve to be a person of greatness? Are you less worthy than anyone else? I hope you say that you are not less worthy but if you did, you need to know the truth is that you are not less worthy than anyone else even though you have made mistakes.

Your greatness is also about being truthful to yourself and knowing that we all make mistakes but that does not make us less worthy and we deserve to live in positivity and to be optimized in life.

Activity 3.5

> *"If we learn to open our hearts, anyone, including the people who drive us crazy, can be our teacher."*
>
> —*Pema Chodron*

Accepting others for who they are, even those who treat us badly, helps us to think rationally and also helps us to make smarter choices related to who we follow or who we choose to stop hanging out with. This concept can sound a little bizarre at first because we could ask, "Why would I accept that some people will treat me unfairly?" Well the truth is because they can treat you unfairly. Right? People can be mean, cruel and even violent toward other people. That is a choice they make. When we accept people as human beings who make mistakes or bad choices, we accept them first as human beings. The more you become conscious and accept that a person can make the choice to be unfair, the more conscious you will become about making a choice as to whether or not you want to be with that person any longer. (NOTE: If this person is an adult, you need to discuss this with another adult because as a minor, we need to work together against abuse in your life.)

We cannot make a person treat us fairly as every person has the right to make his or her own choices. We cannot impose or force people to do what we want them to do. It is healthier for us to believe that a person who treats us unfairly is not better than or less than other human beings. The truth is that person would benefit from counseling and the lessons we are learning in this workbook, but we cannot force him or her to participate or to change.

Being rational and seeing people as human beings who make mistakes help us to be more accepting of others. It does not mean that we allow others to continue to treat us unfairly, cruelly or abusively. We need to take action to reduce this in our lives. We are not accepting of the unfair treatment, cruelty or abusive behavior, but we are being realistic that people will behave this way…some more than others.

KEY POINTS

Unconditional Other-Acceptance:

1. **Other people will treat me unfairly from time to time.**

2. **There is no reason why they must treat me fairly.**

3. **The people who treat me unfairly are no more worthy and no less worthy than any other human being.**

> "You can't always get what you want, but if you try
> sometimes, you might find, you get what you need."
>
> —*Mick Jagger*

Sometimes life can seem very unfair and sometimes it truly is. Albert Ellis was known for teaching us how to **stay sane in a crazy world**. I know these concepts can be very hard to swallow when people deal with brutality, abuse, war and injustices like racism and hate crimes. For the most part, Ellis teaches us that we need to understand and accept that people act inappropriately and make bad choices. When we accept this we are better off because then we can deal with life without making things worse for ourselves. If we tell ourselves people MUST not act this way, we are not being realistic because throughout history people have done really mean, hurtful and brutal things to one another. The truth is we would *prefer* to have a world without these crimes, but that is not the reality.

> "I think it's unfair, but they have the right as fallible, screwed-
> up humans to be unfair; that's the human condition."
>
> —*Mick Jagger*

KEY POINTS

Unconditional Life-Acceptance:

1. Life doesn't always work out the way that I'd like it to.

2. There is no reason why life must go the way I want it to.

3. Life is not necessarily pleasant but it is never awful and is nearly always bearable.

Rational Thinking: How to Stay Sane in a Crazy World

Activity 4.1 — Activity 4.2

Positivity & Rational

Although we adults have been teaching these things for a long time, it does not mean that we think they are easy. We also practice what we preach and sometimes I can say that I have to apply MASSIVE Resets to myself. You will be learning about Reset and The Dancing Toll Taker soon. We all have to practice seeing how the toll taker sees things and works hard on appreciating beauty and counting things to be grateful for. We know that doing these things helps you achieve that goal.

We also realize that it is normal for us to experience negative emotions and there is a difference between healthy and unhealthy negative emotions. You may remember that in the beginning I told you about using the Nurtured Heart Approach® as "Miracle-Grow" in real life with other techniques. Now that you have been practicing and learning about the Nurtured Heart Approach®, the next few lessons will be about how to stay sane in a crazy world. First we will start with the difference between healthy and unhealthy negative emotions.

> "Never apologize for feeling because
> when you do you apologize for truth."
> —*Meryl Streep*

Remember a few lessons ago when we discussed Albert Ellis and Rational Emotive Behavior Therapy (REBT) with Unconditional Self-Acceptance (USA), Unconditional Acceptance of Others (UAO) and Unconditional Life Acceptance (ULA)? We are getting back to a bit of those teachings to learn about healthy negative emotions versus unhealthy negative emotions. Rational Emotive Behavior techniques are also used as coaching techniques. Let's think about this in terms of "life" coaching instead of therapy and the building of your emotional intelligence.

Believe it or not, there is a belief that emotional intelligence can be even more beneficial than having a high IQ. The other added bonus is that when we have better emotional intelligence, we have more friends or social networks because we handle our emotions in a positive and healthy way and also understand the emotions of others. Let's begin with understanding the difference between unhealthy and healthy negative emotions.

Healthy Negative Emotions	Unhealthy Negative Emotions
Disappointment	Shame/Hurt/Embarrassment
Annoyance	Jealousy
Sadness	Depression
Regret	Guilt
High Frustration Tolerance	Low Frustration Tolerance
Concern	Anxiety/Worry
Healthy Anger	Rage/Ongoing Anger

The goal is to stay within the healthy negative emotion range. New studies show that in order to outweigh one negative emotion we need three positive emotions. This means for example that if we are anxious or worried about something, we need to outweigh it with three positive emotions to bring it back down to the healthy negative emotion of concern. To be concerned about something is healthy but when it turns to worry, anxiety or a phobia we are then experiencing an unhealthy negative emotion.

Take a look at the unhealthy negative emotions and write down one you think you could use some help with:

_____

_____

What self-defeating or negative behaviors are attached to this emotion?

_____

_____

Where did that unhealthy negative emotion come from? Did something happen? What event occurred?

_____

Positivity & Rational

By completing the statements, you just did the "A" and "C" of Rational Emotive Behavior Therapy (REBT) or Coaching (REBC). You will learn the "B" in the next section.

A: Identify the "A"ctivating event (Adversity) or thought that is disturbing you.

C: The "C"onsequence identified as the unhealthy negative emotion and self-defeating behaviors that are the result of our irrational beliefs that we hold and energize.

Now let's add some more Miracle-Grow to this concept. By using Kool Kodak and Polaroid Power moments, known as active and experiential recognitions in the Nurtured Heart Approach®, you can outweigh the unhealthy negative emotions.

NURTURED HEART® TIP: Notice and allow yourself to feel the emotion you are feeling. Take action to handle it without causing yourself more disturbance. One action step is doing the self-help form included in this workbook. Write down the strengths you see in yourself for taking this action. Put Polaroid Power into action now and finish this sentence:

I see that by learning this information, I am _____

and I am showing myself that I _____.

I am also _____.

EXAMPLE: I see that by learning this information, I am open-minded and I am showing myself that I have good self-control. I am also determined. Use your own words.

Be proactive with Clarity Canon and use what are known as Proactive Recognitions in the Nurtured Heart Approach®. Use these recognitions when you have a healthy negative emotion and you are handling it and NOT allowing it to go from concern to anxiety, worry and phobias.

Now write down what rule you are not breaking in terms of not allowing your healthy negative emotions to turn into unhealthy negative emotion:

I am not _____.

I could be _____, but I am

making a smart choice to learn something new to help change my thoughts when they are acting as WMDs (Weapons of Mass Destruction otherwise known as Worry, Misery and Doubt).

NURTURED HEART® MIRACLE-GROW: I am not feeding the unhealthy negative emotion of anxiety. I could be sitting around and worrying, but instead I am taking action to help myself. This is good self-care.

Use your own words and write a sentence that applies to your choices:

_____

_____

_____

Now you know some basics of Rational Emotive Behavior techniques. Let's work more on how to get rid of disturbing thoughts, self-defeating behaviors and unhealthy negative emotions.

NURTURED HEART® TIP: By addressing your thoughts you are learning how to change your view like The Dancing Toll Taker that you will learn more about. By not allowing them to turn into unhealthy negative emotions, you are making smart choices to learn a new way to prevent that from happening.

Positivity & Rational

> **"Men are disturbed not by events,**
> **but by the views which they take of them."**
>
> —*2000 years ago, Epictetus, a Greek philosopher*

As you can see by the above quote, human beings have known that the way we see things can disturb us. It is part of our ancient memory as a collective or tribe. The Dancing Toll Taker really is a great example about how a person can see things in a different way. He has a great view that will you hear more about. Even though he would prefer to be a dancer, he is grateful to have a job. He does not make his life at his job miserable because he would rather be a dancer on a stage. He has a healthy view and is grateful to have a job.

Changing our view also changes our thoughts and beliefs. The basic idea in Rational Emotive Behavior teachings is that we have both rational and irrational beliefs. In other words, what is reasonable? What makes sense? What is logical? This is how we would describe the word rational. Irrational, on the other hand, is not reasonable, does not make good sense and can be very illogical.

There are five basic principles that help us decide what is rational and what is irrational.

1. **If I believe a thought to be true, will it help me remain safe, stay in control or bring a positive outcome?**

2. **Can I provide evidence that my opinion or thought is true?**

3. **Is this thought producing feelings I want to have?**

4. **Is this thought helping me reach a chosen goal?**

5. **Is this thought likely to reduce conflict with others?**

When you have a thought that is disturbing you, write it down and then go through the list and answer the questions.

The great news is we can choose to unlearn the five irrational beliefs that many of us hold.

1. **"MUST"ing:** "I must, you must, they must, he/she must" or "I should, you should, they should, he/she should." These are demands that we either make on ourselves or others. For example, "I must succeed and obtain approval." Practice leaving the words "must" and "should" out of your vocabulary.

2. **Awfulizing:** Awfulizing is when we create "drama" and make a situation into a catastrophe or make it worse than it is because we tell ourselves it is the worst thing that could happen in the world. When we exaggerate a situation we are awfulizing. For example, "My parents were arguing about money and were about to kill each other." "My friend is not speaking to me and now I will lose all my other friends." "I was so embarrassed I could have died!"

3. **Low Frustration Tolerance (LFT):** This belief is irrational because we tell ourselves that we cannot stand something but in reality we can. Many teens and adults make this statement: "I can't quit smoking; it would be too hard for me." Think about this: Can you quit lung cancer? Here is another LFT statement: "I cannot stand it when my friends do not include me in an activity."

4. **Rating and Blaming:** "I'm worthless because I made a mistake," or "The world's a rotten place to live." Rating yourself or others as bad, ugly, stupid or better than you is irrational Blaming everything or everyone else for your strong feelings is irrational. "Sarah made me cry today because she would not speak to me," or "My teacher embarrassed me in front of the whole class and it's her fault I am not getting a good grade in that class," or "Eduardo is such a jerk."

5. **Overgeneralizing:** Always or never attitudes. Two more words to drop from your vocabulary are "always" and "never." "You never let me go out!" "I always get punished for everything!"

KEY POINTS

1. **Irrational beliefs are harmful and cloud your mind with distortions, misconceptions, overgeneralizations, and oversimplifications.**

2. **They limit and narrow your outlook on things and force you to keep making the same mistakes over and over.**

3. **Sometimes they act as an escape from reality and stress, and they prevent long-term goal achievement and benefits.**

4. **Core irrational beliefs present in destructive conditions such as impulsiveness, arrogance, defeatism, condemnation, depression, anxiety, hostility, insecurity, addictions, procrastination, prejudice, envy, compulsions, and obsessions.**

Positivity & Rational

You can choose another way and decide to live rationally. Here are 10 awesome reasons to think rationally, be happier and healthier and set the stage to promote your personal growth:

1. We become productive and creative.

2. Positive relationships are built as we encourage acceptance and tolerance of others and ourselves.

3. We learn how to be responsible for our actions without unnecessary blame.

4. Persistence and self-discipline grows stronger.

5. We learn healthy risk-taking.

6. Emotional well-being and positive mental health increases.

7. We are able to have a more realistic point of view.

8. We encourage the empowerment of others.

9. We create an openness to experience and to experiment with new things in a safe way.

10. We are directed toward smart decisions and quickly know right from wrong.

That is a lot of information and you are likely wondering how you can learn in an easy way to think rationally. There is a self-help form on pages 100—104. When something or someone is disturbing or bothering you, you simply need to complete this form to work through your irrational beliefs. This form has blended some Nurtured Heart® techniques that will deepen your experience and anchor it into your mind and heart.

Remember Rafael Reset? He teaches about resetting back to our greatness. In this instance, we reset our minds back to a calm place. Calm minds make better choices. Sometimes when we reset ourselves, we need to do some re-calculating to help us make a good choice and then we start over again.

Think about it like this: Reset, Restore and Restart. Think about how a GPS recalculates when a wrong term is made. It doesn't scream and holler at the driver and it doesn't keep going in the wrong direction. It keeps trying to recalculate to get the driver back on track. Think about how this plan gets you back on track, or if you were off track, it helps you get on the right track.

Rational Emotive Behavior Coaching Form

A (Activating Event or Adversities):

Write down what you are upset about in this moment. What is it that is bothering you? What are you remembering that you keep thinking about? What do you think you have to have right now? What THOUGHTS are you having?

_____

_____

_____

C (Consequences I experience with emotions and behavior):

Check off the unhealthy negative feelings you are having:

- ☐ Depression
- ☐ Anxious/Very Nervous/Worried
- ☐ Feeling Needy
- ☐ Lonely
- ☐ Embarrassed
- ☐ Unhealthy Anger/Rage
- ☐ Hurt
- ☐ Jealous
- ☐ Guilt
- ☐ Very Frustrated/YOU CANNOT STAND IT!

Check off behaviors that cause you trouble in your life. What are you doing?

- ☐ Whining
- ☐ Being Defiant
- ☐ Being Disrespectful
- ☐ Cursing
- ☐ Screaming

Rational Emotive Behavior Coaching Form

☐ **Being Violent**

☐ **Being Violent**

☐ **Shutting Down**

☐ **Ignoring**

☐ **Other(s) (List Below):**

_____

B (Irrational Beliefs):

What are you telling yourself? Complete the sentence(s) that apply.

I MUST _____

_____

I ABSOLUTELY HAVE TO _____

_____

IT'S AWFUL OR TERRIBLE THAT _____

_____

(***This does not include acts of violence or cruel behavior which we all could say is pretty terrible. This means when we make something worse than it is by "awfulizing" or creating unnecessary drama.)

I CANNOT STAND IT WHEN _____

_____

I AM BAD BECAUSE _____

_____

SHE/HE IS BAD BECAUSE _____

_____

Rational Emotive Behavior Coaching Form

I HATE MYSELF WHEN _____

_____

D (Dispute the Irrational Beliefs):

How is it helping you or not helping you to hold the above beliefs? Prove them to be true. Prove it is awful or terrible. Prove you are bad. Prove that you cannot stand it. Does it make sense? The point is you cannot prove them to be true and you can handle it. You also prove that you or another person is not bad because a mistake or a poor choice was made.

_____

_____

_____

E (Effective New Philosophies, Preferences or Beliefs):

Write down what you wish, prefer or want. For example, "It stinks that I cannot go out now but I CAN stand it and make the right choice." "I am a great person who sometimes makes mistakes. I wish I did not but I did and I can learn from them." "I am learning from my mistakes and want to try harder." "I would prefer it if I were allowed to go out and I can choose to show my parents positive behavior to earn the right to go out tomorrow."

_____

_____

_____

E (Effective New Emotions & Behaviors):

Try out new, healthy feelings and behaviors. For example, "I am calm and in control," or "I am respecting my parents and NOT getting into trouble."

Add in a Nurtured Heart® statement:

What rules am I NOT BREAKING? Use a Proactive Recognition in Clarity Canon's style. Actively recognize yourself in a Kool Kodak Moment. I AM STANDING IN MY

Rational Emotive Behavior Coaching Form

GREATNESS and I am making smart choices!!! Write things like this down.

_____

_____

_____

New HEALTHY NEGATIVE FEELINGS. Check off all that apply to you now:

- ☐ **Disappointed NOT frustrated**
- ☐ **Concerned NOT anxious or very nervous**
- ☐ **Sad NOT depressed**
- ☐ **Annoyed NOT angry**
- ☐ **Regretful NOT guilty**
- ☐ **A Little Frustrated/YOU CAN STAND IT! You are handling your strong feelings!**

ENERGIZE YOUR SUCCESS with an Experiential Recognition, or a Polaroid Power Moment. Write down how smart, safe, respectful and in control you are right now in this moment. Be sincere. Write things down that you truly believe about yourself in this moment. What strengths, values and virtues are you showing yourself and others?

_____

_____

_____

_____

Rational Emotive Behavior Coaching Form

SMALL GROUP ACTIVITY: Play Let's Get Rational and be sure as you play that you are all using Nurtured Heart® Recognition Exercises as described in full below.

> **"Grant me the serenity to accept the things I cannot change, the courage to change the things that I can, and the wisdom to know the difference."**

Discuss this as a group and the deeper meaning of these words. Share with us what you discuss on **tribalwarriorsblog.com**.

What do you know that you cannot control or change?

_____

_____

How can you gain courage to change something you do have control over changing?

_____

_____

How can you gain more wisdom to help you make these kinds of decisions?

_____

_____

Amping Up with Positive Psychology

Activity 5.1 — Activity 5.6

Activity 5.1

> **"With Positivity, you'll learn to see new possibilities, bounce back from setbacks, connect with others, and become the best version of yourself."**
>
> **—Barbara Fredrickson**

According to the Merriam-Webster Encyclopedia Britannica, the first known use of this word goes back to 1659 in the 17th century. Can you even imagine what life was like over 400 years ago? If you want to, Google that time period. It was very different—extremely different from the world as we know it today. BUT, the common thread that pulls us back to that time and since then is that we talked about positivity. Let's face it…for most of us, if not all of us, when asked if you would choose positivity over negativity, most of us would choose positivity. A no-brainer, right?

List three things that remind of you positivity:

1. _____
2. _____
3. _____

It was discovered by Barbara Fredrickson that we need three positive emotions to one negative emotion to get us to a point where we tip the scales in our favor. When this happens we naturally become stronger inside and are more resilient meaning we can bounce back quicker. We are able to deal with difficult situations and we easily achieve more than we can imagine.

Some people get very confused when they hear things like this. It does not mean that because you can outweigh a negative emotion with three positive emotions that gives you or anyone else a good reason to hurt others, for example, with mean words and then go back and say three nice things to undo it. What this really means is that we need much more positive emotion to lift us up to outweigh the negative emotion. Think about it like this, negative emotion is heavier than positive emotion and it drags you down.

This discovery proves that it makes sense to practice and use the things we are teaching you in this workbook. It is really good for you. When you do the Nurtured Heart® Activities and notice yourself, you are installing new software in the form of positive emotions and building strengths, or your inner wealth.

If it is hard for you to *be positive*, don't force it. Sometimes many of us do not feel positive or do not even want to be positive because we may be depressed, angry or very frustrated with the way our life is going or with the people in it. It is understandable that for many people living in very difficult situations that it can be hard to find a way to be positive and I want us all to respect and accept that in others. I can tell you that if you are one of those people, it would help your situation if you made a choice to try these things out.

If you try to force it, you will create more negativity within you. Try these three steps:

1. Create the mindset by being open, appreciative, curious and kind to yourself and others.

2. BE REAL. Don't fake it. This is not a situation to fake it until you make it.

3. Notice yourself using the Nurtured Heart® Activities when you are in this place.

EXAMPLE: "I notice that even though it is hard to be positive, I am thinking about it and learning about it. That says a lot about me making smart choices for myself." Write down your own statement. What do you notice about yourself now?

_____

_____

_____

_____

What's LOVE Got to Do With It?

It has been revealed that love is our supreme emotion. Although most of us think about romantic love or love toward our family or friends, love goes much deeper and wider than that. "Love effects everything we think, feel do and become" according to Barbara Fredrickson. When you are willing to increase positivity in your life, you are able to accept more love in your life, and this helps you become more connected with others at home, school, in your friendships, with teams and in your communities.

Believe it or not, having more love and positivity in your life really changes the cells in your bodies. Everyone is better off for it. We increase a hormone called oxytocin and when we do not only do we get more brain power, every cell in our body is optimized and we are better able to connect and relate to others. Discuss with your group or with the person you are working with why this can be a good thing in your life. What are your thoughts? Blog them on **tribalwarriorsblog.com**

Activity 5.3

> "People who learn to control inner experience
> will be able to determine the quality of their lives,
> which is as close as any of us can come to being happy."
>
> —*Mihaly Csikszentmihalyi,*
> *Flow: The Psychology of Optimal Experience, 1990*

There are studies in what is known as the psychology of optimal experience. Basically this means when we get really involved in something, or "in the zone" and we are excited about that experience, we are optimized and completely engaged in life. We are not going to teach this entire experience but if you want to learn more about it, ask the person working with you and do a research project on how powerful this is for you and others.

For now, we want to teach you how to get into flow. Remember the signature strengths you did earlier in this workbook? It has been discovered that when you engage in activities that are related to your signature strengths, that you can get into a state of flow, or get in the zone.

Pick one of your signature strengths from that lesson and write it down here:

_____

_____

_____

Think about activities that you would like to do that are connected to that signature strength.

Be creative with this activity. Write down at least three (more if you can):

1. _____

2. _____

3. _____

4. _____

5. _____

6. _____

Get into the habit of finding ways to increase your flow through life. Keep in mind that your interests and strengths can change over time. Stay in tune with that. It is a great idea to do your signature strengths over time to see how they change as you grow and change. This is a life practice…not just a teenage practice.

Positivity & Rational

> "Plenty of people miss their share of happiness, not because they never found it, but because they didn't stop to enjoy it."
>
> —*William Feather*

There is an activity called *Savoring* that I learned about from Dr. Seligman many years ago. He suggested that we are caught up in rushing through life that we have forgotten how to appreciate things and we take things for granted. Think about it this way: write down what your favorite food is to eat. It can be something sweet, fast food or a home cooked meal. Pick something that you know you can have this week. If you can, do this with the person or the group you are working with on this workbook.

Favorite Food(s):

_____

_____

_____

When you can have this food, take the time to really enjoy it. Allow yourself to smell the food and chew it slowly. Take the time to enjoy it. Spend two to three minutes thinking about, smelling, tasting and experiencing the food in your mouth. Don't rush to eat it. Slow down. Write about this experience in your journal and learn how to slow down more in life instead of rushing or worrying about what is the next thing you need to do in life.

Now write down something that you enjoy. For example, do you like it when the sun is shining? You may even like it when it is raining, as it may remind you of the earth getting its own shower.

_____

_____

_____

Practice savoring with this too. This is not a onetime activity and this is something that we suggest you learn how to do regularly. This is also about staying in the moment, in the kNOWing and allowing all your senses to savor and appreciate what you are doing.

Savoring Greatness Activity

Be sure you are keeping a daily list of your TGTs (Three Greatness Things). Every evening before you go to sleep, savor your greatness by looking at that list and reflecting back on all the positivity you experienced. Think about the good sensations you had in your body and the positive emotions and thoughts that are connected to those TGTs. Let's practice one here.

List one TGT:

_____

What positive emotion is attached to this?

_____

How does this feel in your body? For example, excited, calm, etc.?

_____

What positive and rational thoughts do you have?

_____

_____

Take this a little deeper and practice calm breathing. Pull this greatness into your heart as you learn how to enjoy the art of savoring greatness.

There's an old Cherokee teaching story where an elder tells his grandson, "Within all people, a battle goes on between two wolves. One is negativity—anger, sadness, stress, contempt, disgust, fear, embarrassment, guilt, shame, and hate. The other is positivity—joy, gratitude, serenity, interest, hope, pride, amusement, inspiration, awe, and—above all—love." The grandson asks, "Which wolf wins?" and the old Cherokee replies, "The one you feed."

Positivity & Rational

> "**What you focus on expands, and when you focus on
> the goodness in your life, you create more of it.
> Opportunities, relationships, even money flowed my way
> when I learned to be grateful no matter what happened in my life.**"
>
> —*Oprah Winfrey*

Back in 2003, I learned about a powerful activity that touches the heart and soul of people you know, care for and love. It is called a Gratitude Visit. We are going to amp this up by adding qualities of greatness in a Nurtured Heart® way. You are being encouraged to adopt an attitude of gratitude not only for this little section but through life. If you and your family practice a religion and use prayer, this will sound familiar in the form of counting your blessings and thanking a higher power in your life.

Google the word "attitude." What do you learn?

_____

_____

Google the word "gratitude." What do you learn?

_____

_____

Let's Get to it with a Gratitude and Greatness Visit

Think of the people—parents, friends, teachers, coaches, teammates, employers, and so on—who have been especially kind to you but whom you have never properly thanked. Choose someone with whom you could arrange to have a face-to-face meeting in the next week. You could also pick someone that you cannot meet with but can either Skype or call on the telephone. Write their name down:

_____

Write down all the greatness you see in them. Write down their strengths and the positivity you see. Be specific and use details about how they show this to you. Write as if you are speaking right to them. Use "I see" or "I notice" and "You are" statements.

_____

_____

Your task is to write a gratitude and greatness letter to this individual and deliver it in person or on Skype or the telephone by reading it aloud. Be specific about what he or she did for you and how it affected or changed your life. What did you learn from them?

_____

_____

_____

Let the person know what you are doing now and mention how often you remember their efforts. Directly following the gratitude and greatness visit, take some time to reflect on the experience:

How did you feel as you wrote the letter?

_____

_____

_____

How did the other person react to your expression of gratitude?

_____

_____

_____

How were you affected by their reaction?

_____

_____

_____

Positivity & Rational

> "Positive psychology is more interested in how to turn a good relationship into an excellent one."
>
> —*Dr. Martin Seligman*

I cannot express how powerful language is and today we are having many challenges communicating because we are more often communicating virtually with texting, emailing, instant messages and on many virtual platforms like Facebook, for example. Communicating virtually is not going to go away anytime soon and we are able to communicate with more people than ever before. That comes with its good points and its bad points. We are asking you to practice with the way you use language both verbally and virtually. In the next activity, we fully explain how to use the Nurtured Heart Approach® as a powerful way to use language through recognizing positivity and greatness in yourself and others. In this section, we are going to learn Dr. Martin Seligman's teachings for constructing sentences. He teaches us four ways that we can respond to others and only one combination builds relationships: the *Active and Constructive Response*. The four ways are *Active, Constructive, Passive and Destructive*. We also want you to learn how to apply this to yourself as it relates to your self-talk. Let's start with the one we want you to use and practice. We will give examples for applying it to yourself and others for each concept.

Active and Constructive Response

Let's define these two terms. "Active" is when we take action, when we actively participate we are energetically alive in a situation. "Constructive" is similar to building something up. How do we construct something? Think about a building being constructed. Each part of the construction has a useful purpose. Here is an example to apply to yourself: Positive Event: You receive a good grade on your biology test.

Active and Constructive Thought:

"Wow. I am proud of myself. I needed that grade to change my average in that class."

Active and Constructive Replay:

Think about the positive feelings you are experiencing in the moment. Are you happy, excited and filled with a sense of pride? Take some more action and share this great news with your friends and family.

Now let's imagine that your friend approaches you and tells you about the good grade they got. Here is how you respond in an **Active and Constructive Response:**

"That's awesome. I know you were worried about that class. What did your teacher say? Did you tell your family yet? Where were you when you got the news? How good do you feel right now? Hey, we should celebrate by doing something fun this weekend."

Nonverbal Active and Constructive Response:

- Pay attention

- Make eye contact

- Be genuine and show positive emotion, like smiling, laughing, or a pat on the back

Let's try it out now. Write down a real or imagined positive event that you personally experienced:

_____

_____

Write down your Active and Constructive Thought about the event:

_____

_____

What positive feelings do you have as you think about it now in this moment?

_____

_____

Who are you going to tell? Include anyone and everyone.

_____

_____

Positivity & Rational

Make a copy of this form and keep it with you to help get you in the practice of using Active and Constructive Responses at home, school and in down time with friends or in activities such as sports, dance, etc.

My Positive Event	My Exact Active and Constructive Thought	Positive Feelings & Who I Will Tell

Use this section to notice other's positive events. To start practicing, think back to some good news someone shared with you. Write it down below and practice how you would respond with this new information. Keep this form next to your bed or somewhere that you will notice it so when you wake up, you think about how you can be active and constructive throughout your day.

My Positive Event	My Exact Active and Constructive Thought	Positive Feelings & Who I Will Tell

Now, here is what **_NOT_** to do. The next three responses are:

Passive and Constructive Response:

"Good news. You deserve it," or "Oh good, you did well on the test." There is little enthusiasm or expressed interest. You don't say or think anything else about the positive event.

Active and Destructive Response:

"Oh now I know why you have not been hanging out with us so much" or "Okay brainiac… guess we won't be seeing you this weekend." We can sound sarcastic and unsupportive in this response.

Passive and Destructive Response:

This is completely ignoring what the person is sharing with you and there is no acknowledgement about the positive event. An example would be, "Where are we hanging out after school?"

REMEMBER: Use *Active and Constructive Responses* to build strong relationships and stop using the last three responses, which can destroy relationships. The next section teaches us how to take it up a notch to nurture healthy and positive relationships.

The Heat is On:
The Nurtured Heart® Foundations

Activity 6.1 — Activity 6.6

The Heat is On

The Nurtured Heart Approach® is about building inner wealth in relationships. When we relate to others, we can use its tools to see greatness and to talk about what we see.

What does the word "relate" mean to you?

_____

_____

What positive relationships do you have now?

_____

_____

We can use those same tools to see and talk about greatness in ourselves. You learn to develop the ability to see and to describe in detail what you see. It sounds easy but does take practice to change. To make this happen, you'll learn about one approach with:

- Four foundational concepts (in this section)

- Three "warrior" stands (remember they were previously mentioned in the Preface)

- Four techniques (three of them have camera nicknames)

The concepts support the stands; together, they'll provide you with the basic information to understand the approach. Once you've learned those concepts and stands, the techniques give you the tools to *live and speak* this approach and to teach it to others. The key is to learn how to apply it to yourself.

The Language of Greatness

Think about it as learning a new language. When you learn a new language, not only do you learn how to say the alphabet or to count numbers in that language, you learn about the culture and how to live within that culture. You communicate, behave and even see things differently than you would from your native culture. When you learn the Nurtured Heart Approach®, you begin to live life very differently. You see, feel, speak and think in a different way that builds your inner wealth and greatness. In turn, you build inner wealth and greatness in others. You learn the *language of greatness*.

Don't worry too much about grasping this right now. Let's jump right into those foundational concepts, which might seem a little silly or random at first. Be patient. It will all fit together as you learn the approach.

This is a wealthy relationship tree showing the roots of Inner Wealth. Fill in the blocks in the positive family and friends tree of greatness. Be sure to write the names of the people and the things that make them great—their positive qualities and strengths.

The Heat is On

Four Foundational Concepts

*1. **We are the toys.*** Think about the famous toy store "Toys R Us."

We learn at a very young age how to create relationships and get attention. In fact, we are born with that power. There is a pretty funny YouTube video called, "Why waste a temper tantrum when no one is around to see it?" If you can, watch it now. This little toddler shows great self-control. When his mother is not in the room, he immediately stops his tantrum. He then searches for her and the second he finds her he immediately throws himself back in temper tantrum behavior. He is lighting up with negative behavior, however his parents are not responding to it. He likely wants something he cannot have and was told the word "no."

What do you normally do when you are told no?

_____

_____

Be honest, do you try to bother your parents or to annoy someone so much to get what you want?

_____

_____

For children, parents or caregivers, teachers and other adults are their favorite toys. No other toy can match what they can do. They express countless emotions, expressions and energies in response to children's behaviors. Children watch carefully from infancy to see what their favorite toys do in response to their choices, both good and bad. Adults "light up" with sounds and actions teaching us how to get what we want or to get the attention we want. This is how children learn to behave in the world.

As social beings and as teenagers we continue to require love and attention from friends, teachers, and family members. Sometimes we make stories more dramatic or may even flat out lie to get attention or to make friends or make people laugh. In fact it is pretty safe to say that mostly everyone has done this at least once in their lifetime. In more serious situations, some of us act out violently either physically or with abusive language.

ONTO THE NEXT LEVEL

Name a time when you made up a story or gave it more drama to either make someone laugh, to make a friend or perhaps to get out of trouble:

_____

_____

What was the outcome? How did the person respond to your story?

_____

_____

Have you ever wanted to hurt someone because they hurt you? Not physically but with words.

_____

_____

Were you successful? Did you make them angry or cry?

_____

_____

In these instances you were lit up like a toy…like a video game and they were lit up as well but all related to negative experiences.

In Nurtured Heart® language, we are asking you to turn this upside down. From now on, we do not feed negative energy or drama by lighting up, responding to or acting out our own negative thoughts or behaviors from others. We do light up by taking action to handle those negative thoughts or behaviors in a healthy and safe way.

It is natural for you as a teenager to seek feedback and reinforcement in the form of energy and attention. In this way, we can think of ourselves as "toys" from which we want to get and give as many energized relationships as possible.

When we find ways to see and verbally acknowledge success—or, as Dr. G would say, _energize_ success—we come to recognize when we light up and make fun sounds in response our good choices.

The Heat is On

Write down a negative thought or behavior you believe you would like to change:

_____

_____

 KEYS TO SUCCESS

Find ways to give energy, response and relationship to the good stuff. Focus on what is going strong instead of what is going wrong.

2. Shamu: Catching Success and Goodness vs. Creating Success and Greatness

Have you had the pleasure of seeing an orca whale leap over a rope in a marine park performance? If you have, you might have wondered how human beings have been able to persuade a 30,000 pound killer whale— the most famous of which was Shamu, a female orca whale who was trained to perform at the original Sea World in the 1960s—to do this kind of trick. Many more orca performers have been given the same name and they continue to perform at Sea World parks. As it turns out, the tricks used to train Shamu can be applied to human behavior in both private and public sectors. (Check out some Shamu acts on YouTube.)

If you think that Shamu's training involves being lured over the rope with a food reward, you're right. The key here is the placement of the rope.

Do the trainers start with the rope high in the air? No—because the chances of getting Shamu to leap for a fish right off the bat are slim. Do they put the rope along the surface of the water, perhaps? Just beneath the surface? No on both counts. The trainers wisely lay the rope as low as they possibly can: along the very bottom of the pool.

Once the rope is placed, the trainers wait for Shamu to cruise across it on her own. As soon as she does, she receives plenty of energized rewards in the forms of food and affection. With consistent rewards, given each time Shamu crosses the rope, this highly intelligent creature soon learns to get those rewards from her human friends by crossing the rope on purpose. Once that connection is made, the rope is raised a little bit more each time…and eventually, although it's stretched high above the pool, Shamu continues to show her power and leaps over it so that she can receive those rewards.

This speaks to the importance of energizing, rewarding, and celebrating success every step of the way starting with you and toward others. It speaks to the importance of putting your imaginary rope at the bottom of the pool: of finding ways to create success starting with you!

If we set our expectations too high and fail to notice ourselves and others moving toward a goal, even when we are not soaring and flying high, we miss many chances to nurture greatness. And if we bring negative energy into our daily lives and put ourselves or others down when we fail to soar to great heights of achievement we create an environment of negativity.

The Nurtured Heart Approach® gives us tools for seeing and acknowledging success, no matter what. Every time Shamu swims over that rope—no matter how low it lies beneath the water—success is created. The NHA teaches us to take every opportunity to create successes that would otherwise not exist. If we find ways to honor ourselves and others for what isn't wrong, we have a whole lot more to celebrate.

Write down your Shamu for today:

_____

_____

What can you Shamu in someone else?

_____

_____

🔑 KEYS TO SUCCESS

Reinforce and energize yourself and others for following rules; for showing good judgment; for living values like thoughtfulness, responsibility, respectfulness, conscientiousness, creativity, or generosity. Even small successes leads to further success, and before you know it, you are leaping to ever-greater heights of energized success.

The Heat is On

3. Toll Taker: Choosing the Way We See Things

Dr. G shares a story about a dancing toll taker on the San Francisco Bay Bridge. The professor who originally told Dr. G this story reported that he had driven over to the dancer's lane to pay his toll. "It looks like you're having the time of your life," the professor said to the toll taker. The toll taker replied, "Of course! I have the best job in the world and the best office in the world." He colorfully describes the beautiful views he drinks in daily. He gets to see sunrises and sunsets while on the job—and, as luck would have it, he's an aspiring dancer who gets paid to practice in his glass-walled office high above the water! When the professor inquires about the other toll takers who don't seem so energized, the dancing toll taker responds, "Oh, those guys in the stand-up coffins? They're no fun!"

We get to choose how we see things. The toll taker could have focused on the difficult aspects of his job: long days on his feet, car pollution or grumpy drivers. That's what the guys in the stand-up coffins are likely focusing on. He chooses, instead, to focus on what's right about where he is and what he's doing. The best part is that we get to make this choice in any moment of any day. No matter how much we've focused on the negative in the past, each new moment is an opportunity to see and acknowledge what's right in our worlds and in those around us.

ACTIVITY: Choosing to focus on what's right is about getting out of the way and allowing problems to solve themselves. By making this choice, we set intentions to climb to ever-greater heights of success instead of being stuck in unhealthy negativity.

What is one thing that you find yourself focusing on that is not positive?

_____

_____

_____

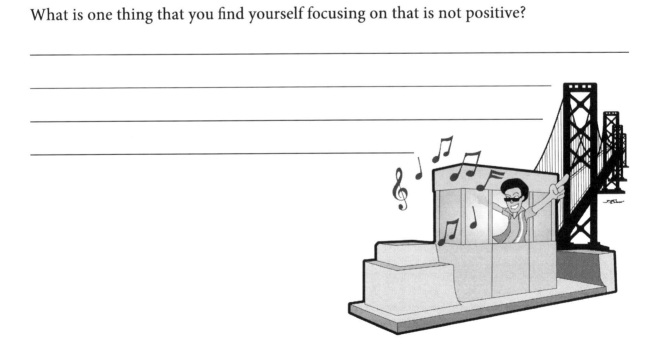

How can you change your view? Can you look at this challenge through another camera lens and come in from another angle? Write down your thoughts. (If you are stuck, no worries. You can work on this in your group or with the person teaching you these concepts.)

_____

_____

KEYS TO SUCCESS

Take a picture of this moment in your mind. See, appreciate, and acknowledge every aspect of the greatness of what you see. Know that the more willing you are to choose to see greatness, the more greatness will come your way.

Go to **values.com** and go to "TV Commercials." Scroll down until you see "The Greatest." Or click on "Optimism" to find it. You will see a boy in a baseball cap. Below is the description from their website but before you read that, watch the one minute video first. Watch it now and think about how he changed his view like the toll taker does at his job.

> The Greatest is all about perspective. Just when you think you are failing, when things seem to be going wrong…a change of perspective shines a bright light of realization that you just might be succeeding in other ways. It is a very simple concept but the key, of course was finding the right young actor to play the part. As you have seen, he is amazing. After countless takes throwing the ball up and missing—which is harder than you might think—he never lost his zeal. The last scene was as strong as the first. "Celebration" by Kool and The Gang fittingly takes us from despair at 'strike three" to euphoria and inspires us to embrace the value of Optimism as we face similar situations each day. After all, you might just be… The Greatest. —values.com

You are the greatest in the world! Remember that. There is no one else in this entire world exactly like you. You are unique and you have great talents…some that you do not even know about at the moment.

The Heat is On

Write down a statement about your greatness. Be dramatic with it. Even if you do not truly believe it, make believe you are acting it out on stage. Get animated with the description.

Write about you being The Greatest _____ in the world!

_____

_____

_____

4. Game Theory: Clear Rules, Clear Consequences and Right Back in the Game of Greatness!

You are the leader of your life and you if you do not set strict and clear limits and enforce rules for yourself and those around you, you will allow rule-breaking and will have many struggles with boundaries around rules. Here are some questions to ask yourself:

- Do you have a hard time standing up for yourself?

- Is it hard to stand up for others when you see someone being treated badly?

- Do you agree to do things that you really don't want to do? Do you just go along with others?

- Do you put up with mean comments or pushy people because you can't handle conflict?

- Do you take things personally?

> **"It is impossible to have a healthy relationship with someone who has no boundaries, with someone who cannot communicate directly and honestly. Learning how to set boundaries is a necessary step in learning how to be a friend to ourselves. It is our responsibility to care for ourselves—to protect ourselves when it is necessary. It is impossible to learn to be loving to ourselves without owning our self—and owning our rights and responsibilities as co-creators of our lives."**
>
> **—Robert Burney**

Think about the answers on the previous page and respond below:

What is a personal boundary for you?

_____

_____

What rule is attached to that boundary?

_____

_____

EXAMPLE: "My boundary is I will only be friends with people who are kind and respect others."

RULE: "I will not accept people threatening me or calling me names. If this happens I will take immediate healthy action to stand up for myself and I will report this to an adult I trust."

Game theory in the NHA is about clearly enforcing rules without giving energy to rule-breaking. This, together with the goal to energize success, is the Nurtured Heart Approach®'s *default setting*. When we energize success and refuse to energize negativity we default back to greatness.

KEYS TO SUCCESS

We choose to clearly define rules and to refuse to energize the breaking of rules (or the pushing of boundaries around rules). When consequences are necessary, we take action calmly and without giving energy or drama. We now get excited when we notice ourselves or others sticking to our boundaries and not breaking rules!

The Heat is On

Believe In Yourself and Your Ability to Make a Change in Your Life

If the idea of making a shift to positivity in your life sounds like a good one, first you need to change *your* mind. Right now. You need to set your intention to start seeing what's right and what's going strong instead of what's wrong in your life.

Here's the good news: just by reading this far, you already *are* proving that your intention is to change the way you see things. But this shift to positivity is deeper than you may think. To truly achieve that pulse of positivity in your life, you'll need to work against the hardwiring of your brain. Believe it or not, our brains take information in much like a computer and store it like saved documents. Just like a saved document, you can change it.

Do you have a fear of snakes? What about spiders? Rodents? For people who fear these creatures, even a photograph of one—or the *thought* of one—can be enough to trigger a classic fight-or-flight response. Evolutionary psychology that studies how our minds and behaviors change or evolve over time teaches that these kinds of fears are part of our hardwiring, which is programmed to notice any hint of danger. The part of the brain that triggers fear is primitive and dates back to when we were cave people.

Our brain does not recognize that a photograph of a spider isn't dangerous or that a pet mouse or snake in a cage will not do harm. It also can't understand that the worries, miseries, and doubts of everyday life are not actual threats to life.

🔑 KEYS TO SUCCESS

The new fight-or-flight: Fight to change your way of thinking. Fight for shifting your mind toward positivity and step back and savor that flight to success as you transform yourself and the world around you. Be grateful for the changes in you that are the changes you wish to see.

We don't want to change that part of the brain, because in times of true danger, it's absolutely necessary. Healthy negative emotions are important for emotional and social well-being. Without healthy anger and frustration, we would not be able to tell the difference between right and wrong. Without these emotions, it would be hard for us to find the energy to fight for justice and speak out about wrongdoing.

Get into your Frontal Lobes

In order to allow the positivity pulse to move through us, we need to make a habit of tapping into the higher-functioning parts of the brain—the frontal lobes, which handles what is called our *executive function*. Executive function allows us to be selective about what we pay attention to or how we plan our behaviors or actions. We get to choose the way we respond to whatever happens to us, and apply our intelligence to solving problems.

Step into your frontal lobes. Give more power to this part of your brain in order to be the change you want to see. In Nurtured Heart® terms we want you to zero in on *what is going right*. It's up to you to take this information to learn how to do this.

Are you ready to choose positivity for your life at home, school and play?

_____

If you said YES, that means you are making a decision that empowers your mind and heart to apply the stands and recognitions you'll learn about in the next sections of this book.

If you said NO or you are unsure, notice how honest you are being in this moment and believe it or not that is you being in control of your mind and your decisions. It also means you are taking a stand about what you want for your life. Think about this. If you do not choose positivity for your life, than what do you choose?

There are many words that you can use to describe what YOU want in your life. Write them down here:

_____

_____

_____

Be the CEO of your life. You are the Chief Executive Officer of your life by Choosing Excellence and Optimization!

The Heat is On

Think back to when you first started reading this workbook. In the explanation we explored the meaning of a Tribal Warrior and found out what they are fighting for. In case you cannot remember here they are again. This tribe holds to the principles of the following three stands. In other words this is what they fight for in warrior-like fashion:

Stand One:

Refuse to Energize Negativity ("Absolutely NO!")

Stand Two:

Relentlessly Energize the Positive. ("Absolutely YES")

Fiercely recognize what is going strong rather than what is going wrong.

Create success and positivity any chance you get.

Stand Three:

Clearly and Unenergetically Enforce Limits. (Absolute Clarity)

Set up clear limits and stick to strict consequences when those rules are broken.

Maintain personal boundaries with a clear code of conduct.

The stands are the support system of this approach. Any time you aren't sure how to react or act, checking back in with your three stands will give you direction and resolve. The skills described in the following section all work to uphold these stands.

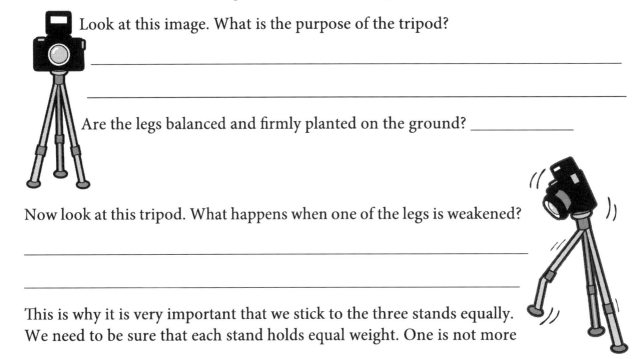

Look at this image. What is the purpose of the tripod?

_____

_____

Are the legs balanced and firmly planted on the ground? _____

Now look at this tripod. What happens when one of the legs is weakened?

_____

_____

This is why it is very important that we stick to the three stands equally. We need to be sure that each stand holds equal weight. One is not more important than the other. They work together in balance with one another and the result is more positivity in your life.

Stand One: Refuse to give any attention or energy to negative behavior and unhealthy negative emotion. 100% refusal.

Remember before about fight-or-flight? Our primal brain, or caveman brain, is wired to fight-or-flight. There is still a piece of that information hard-wired in our brains and in times of trouble, we need it. BUT, we do not need it when it comes to conflicts because if we fight back in this way with more negativity, we are simply putting more gasoline on the fire.

Now there is a new flight and fight. We also fight for opting to do the right thing and encouraging others to do the right thing.

Positivity Peer Pressure

ACTIVITY: Go to **values.com**. Click on "TV Commercials" and Select "Peer Pressure."

> **"Peer Pressure can be used as a positive force."**
> —*The Foundation for a Better Life*

Is that what you expected to happen? _____

What are your thoughts about turning peer pressure around?

_____

_____

What did you notice about the stand they took in this video?

_____

_____

Did they lecture their friend? _____

What is the clear limit and consequence that they stated in the video?

_____

_____

The Heat is On

What is an Energy or Negativity Leak?

It's happening any time you show that:

- Problems, issues, and broken rules hold your interest

- You expect someone to do something wrong

- You are willing to focus energy and attention on poor choices

- You ignore when a rule is broken or avoid confronting it

Leaking negativity weakens the power of the Nurtured Heart Approach®. The truth is everybody leaks. Even if we do not act out on a negativity leak, sometimes our thoughts go to negativity about what we tell ourselves. We cannot be perfect and it is normal for this to happen but if we feed it, we make it worse. We all make mistakes and leak negative energy.

Can you think of a time when you were leaking negativity?

_____

_____

Did the situation get better or worse by you feeding the negativity? What happened?

_____

_____

Remember the story about the Cherokee grandfather and the story of "The Wolves Within Us."

> *There's an old Cherokee teaching story where an elder tells his grandson, "Within all people, a battle goes on between two wolves. One is negativity—anger, sadness, stress, contempt, disgust, fear, embarrassment, guilt, shame, and hate. The other is positivity—joy, gratitude, serenity, interest, hope, pride, amusement, inspiration, awe, and—above all—love." The grandson asks, "Which wolf wins?" and the old Cherokee replies, "The one you feed."*

REMEMBER: *It's how we bounce back from that mistake or leaking that makes the difference. As soon as you notice a leak, you can change course and step cleanly into a new moment of positivity. The techniques described in the sections on Recognitions will show you how.*

Stand Two: Fiercely recognize what is going strong rather than what is going wrong. Create success and positivity any chance you get.

Be ferocious like a lion! This is a strategy that creates new patterns of positivity, success and greatness.

What are your first thoughts about this stand?

_____

_____

_____

Write down one thing that you see as a strength of yours right in this moment. I notice:

_____

_____

Take it deeper. What does that mean about you? For example, "I notice I am learning something new." To take it deeper: "…and that shows me that I am making a choice to make changes in my life; it shows I am using my intelligence to learn; it shows my willingness to participate in this activity, etc." Now take it deeper for your statement above:

_____

_____

_____

KEY POINTS

1. **In taking the first stand, we commit to refusing to give energy to negativity choosing instead to reset ourselves and others to the greatness that's is in us all from birth.**

2. **Reset gets us back on track and helps us avoid bigger consequences.**

3. **In taking the second stand, we give energy to success, strengths and smart choices no matter what.**

4. **In taking the third stand, we make a commitment to enforce rules strictly but not in a punishing way.**

The Heat is On

When we stick to these three stands with confidence, the energy within you and all around you will change.

Shamu and the Toll Taker: Think back to the stories of Shamu and the toll taker. We set the rope as low as we like in order to catch and create successful moments.

What is one thing that you think you want to work on to increase more success and positivity in your life?

_____

_____

_____

_____

By writing this down, you are setting an intention to make it happen! Good for you! We get to choose how we see things—whether we see what's right and strong instead of what's wrong.

Write down something that you believe you see as always being a downer:

_____

_____

_____

With this new information, how can you begin to focus on something that is the opposite of that in terms of seeing it from a different view? Go back to the toll taker lesson if you need some extra self-coaching. Write your new view now.

_____

_____

_____

_____

Watch the video again on **values.com** about the boy who changed his perspective, or view on playing baseball.

Stand Three: Set up clear limits and stick to strict consequences when those rules are broken. Maintain personal boundaries with a clear code of conduct.

The Nurtured Heart Approach® is not a "soft" approach. It doesn't mean we are praising ourselves or others when rules are broken. It's about knowing the rules cold; about reinforcing and noticing when we do not break them. We need to be consistent about giving a consequence whenever others break the rules and we need to be clear about what our consequences will be if we choose to break a rule. It's also about moving right on to the next moment of success, just as we do when playing video games or when we're done with the penalty during a sporting event. We don't give attention and energy to the problem of a broken rule—just the opposite, problems get NO DRAMA. Just a *reset* and then an openhearted invitation back to the greatness that was always there.

Whether you are enforcing rules or giving out positive recognitions, you are playing hardball with this approach. You're fiercely nurturing hearts and playing this game to *win!* Take these stands with determination. Be RELENTLESS and FEARLESS about applying this approach. Just as we refuse to forget to energize success (Stand Two), we refuse to look the other way when someone is breaking a rule (Stand Three).

Stating rules in negative language. For example:

- *NO putting myself or others down*
- *NO abusive language*
- *NO hurting myself or others*
- *NO coming in late*
- *NO drama*
- *NO unhealthy negative attitude*
- *NO talking in class*
- *NO sarcastic comments*
- *NO racist, sexist, homophobic, ageist, or religious jokes or comments*
- *NO inappropriate clothing*

Write down three rules that you either have for yourself or know you have to follow at home, school, in sports, or out in the community:

1. _____

2. _____

3. _____

ACTIVITY: Take a moment, right now to appreciate that you are not breaking any of these rules at this time. What does that say about you? What is positive about those choices? You could be interrupting the lesson, you could walk out of group or session, but you are not.

The Heat is On

A personal code of conduct is the rules we make for ourselves that help keep us "in check." Sometimes it is important for us to "check ourselves" if we know we are responding to something with strong and intense feelings. By having our own personal rules, we set up the road map that helps guide our decision making and our behaviors. It also helps us to hold ourselves accountable, or responsible for our actions. Here is an example list.

Every day I will practice:

- Having an attitude of gratitude

- Being respectful and kind toward others

- Taking care of myself in all ways

- Showing compassion to others

- Having fun and laughing

- Practicing greatness, seeing it in myself and others

- Being curious and playful

- Being the leader of my life

- Having faith in myself and in a religion, if that is my belief system

- Noticing that life is a lesson and a journey and every experience teaches us something new about ourselves and the world

Write down your personal code of conduct:

_____

_____

_____

_____

_____

Social Rules

These are the rules that we need to follow in school, at home and in our communities. You already know social rules.

Write down some rules you have at home:

_____

_____

_____

At school:

_____

_____

_____

In your community (laws, etc.):

_____

_____

_____

Think back to the video on Peer Pressure and how the law about not stealing was upheld by the other teenagers. They encouraged their friend to do the right thing and he made a choice with their pressure not to steal the CDs. This is what is meant by having clear rules and sticking to them in all parts of your life.

The Heat is On

You have been using these strategies up to this point with the Nurtured Heart® tips and activities. It sounds easy but it does take practice to change your mindset and behavior to spread positivity all around. These tools help you make that change. They are designed to constantly recognize and notice positivity. Because they involve capturing a moment of success in real time, just as you'd do when snapping a photograph, three of the four are named after cameras.

Strategy 1: Active Recognitions ("Kool" Kodak Moments)

At the Greatness Academy, Kool Kodak is the expert in this strategy. Clearly observe what you are doing in the moment when you are acting positively. Make it a "Kodak moment" by taking a picture of what you see yourself doing. Avoid any kind of judgment. For example:

- "I notice I got up on time today."

- "My friend was really annoying me and I stayed calm and in control."

- "I notice I am working with my group to get this project done."

Write down a Kool Kodak Moment that you see right now in this moment:

_____

_____

Practice on yourself and practice on others:

- "I notice you got here early today."

- "I noticed Xavier was annoying you and you did not flip out on him."

- "I notice I am working with my group to get this project done."

Write down a Kool Kodak Moment that you see right now in this moment:

_____

_____

Imagine it is also like looking in a mirror. We notice exactly what we see and call out the positive things that are shown. When you notice yourself and others in this way, you are calling attention to and appreciating things that we are supposed to be doing—going to school, following rules, and showing positivity.

Kool Kodak Moments

- Use Active Recognition to create Kodak Moments

- Only use for positive moments

- Also use for handling strong intense healthy negative emotions

- Remember the toll taker: if you choose, you can see positivity almost anywhere

- Never use in reference to rule-breaking or negative behavior

- Use to employ neutral, nonjudgmental language to make the message as "digestible" as possible

- Be very specific and give lots of detail

VIRTUAL Kool Kodak Moments: Spread these recognitions like a virus all over Facebook, Myspace, Tumblr, Twitter and over text messages. When you are chatting, be sure to take public notice of the positivity you see!

Strategy 2: Experiential Recognitions (Polaroid Power Moments)

With this strategy, we build on Active Recognitions, or our Kool Kodak Moments. We add a description of the *values* that you see in positive and smart choices that you and others make. With this strategy, capture the moment of *living* values and showing strengths. Through this, we build up and reinforce character strengths and virtues, or better known as our Inner Wealth. Remember the Pyramid of Inner Wealth.

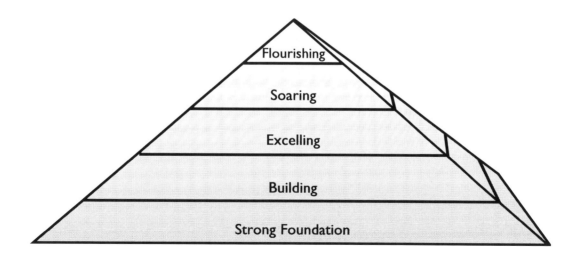

The Heat is On

ACTIVITY: Let's take a moment to be crystal clear that you understand what values, character strengths and virtues are and how they are your Inner Wealth. Google all those terms. Start with values first. Write down what you find:

Values: _____

_____

Name Three Personal Values:

1. _____

2. _____

3. _____

Character Strengths: _____

Rewrite your Five Signature Strengths:

1. _____

2. _____

3. _____

4. _____

5. _____

Virtues/Moral Goodness: _____

Write down three virtues that you already have or would like to have:

1. _____

2. _____

3. _____

Remember these. Write them down on index cards. Make a YouTube video about them. Create a collage or draw about them. Post them on your Facebook wall. Share them with us on **tribalwarriorsblog.com**. Notice these in yourself and others every chance you get! Do activities that build these up even stronger…get OPTIMIZED.

Dr. G describes values as being qualities of your heart. Values, strong character, virtues and moral goodness are behaviors or thoughts judged by society as what is good or what is worthy of imitating. A list of values and strengths worth acknowledging might include:

Compassion	Inventive
Commitment	Kindness
Confidence	Leadership
Consideration	Open-Heartedness
Cooperation	Open-Mindedness
Courage	Patience
Creativity	Peace
Cultural Sensitivity	Resolve
Determination	Resourceful
Expressiveness	Respect
Fairness	Responsibility
Good Sportsmanship	Self-Control
Hardworking	Team Player
Helpfulness	Thoughtfulness
Honesty	Tolerance
Humility	Using Good Manners
Inner Strength	Wisdom

The Heat is On

Experiential Recognition is a right-in-the-moment opportunity to anchor in the values, character strengths, and virtues that you see in yourself and others. Here are some examples for noticing yourself:

- "I notice how hard I am working. I am committed!"

- "I am really angry with Shana, but I am remaining calm."

- "I was very nervous to share my idea with the group, but I did! I am assertive."

Name three Polaroid Power Moments for yourself in this moment. Notice what you are doing and add on the value, character strength or virtue that is attached to that picture:

1. _____

2. _____

3. _____

Here are some examples on how to notice Polaroid Power Moments in others:

- "Juan, I notice how caring you are about your friends. You are kind and a great friend."

- "Michael, you are doing a great job focusing in this group and not texting. You are a team player and showing good self-control."

- "Ashley you are so wonderful about opening up about your feelings in this group. You are really being mature and a great role model for others."

Name three Polaroid Power Moments that you see or remember about others:

1. _____

2. _____

3. _____

NOTE: In the Nurtured Heart Approach®, we stay in the moment, however a picture does not lose its power and it is acceptable to reflect back on positivity.

Experiential Recognitions/Polaroid Power Moment

- Start with a Kool Kodak Moment (Active Recognition) and just notice what you see

- Add a comment that states the value, strength and/or virtue that you see

- Apply this strategy when you or others are doing a great job and/or following the rules

- Be real; show excitement (in your own way)

- Remember Shamu and the toll taker

KEEP SPREADING THE VIRUS: Text someone right now and tell them what you notice about their strengths. BLOG it on **tribalwarriorsblog.com**. Spread it on Facebook.

Strategy 3: Proactive Recognitions (Clarity Canon Moments)

Some of you may think this one is a bit weird. First let's break down the concepts to be sure we have this straight.

What does proactive mean?

_____

_____

Define clarity:

_____

_____

Proactive Recognition builds on the power of Kook Kodak and Polaroid Power, otherwise known as Active and Experiential Recognitions. To proactively recognize yourself or others, you notice and state out loud when you or someone else is *not breaking the rules, overstepping boundaries, feeding negativity, creating drama, or violating your personal code of conduct.*

The Heat is On

Notice right now what rule you are NOT breaking in this moment:

_____

_____

This is what Clarity Canon does. She or he can see very clearly when rules are not being broken and she jumps all over it!

When you celebrate moments where problems are *not* occurring, you are creating more positivity in your life. We do not give energy to broken rules but we do give energy and attention when rules are *not* broken. Rules need to be clear and enforced and we write them beginning with "no." If it is a challenge to start with no, that is okay but they need to be very clear. Let's look at some examples and then you can add some of your own:

- No cell phone use in class

- No being late from free periods or curfew

- No creating drama

- No paying attention to drama

- No gossiping

- No teasing

Write down three other rules that you know from the top of your head:

1. _____

2. _____

3. _____

Let's take a look at Proactive Recognition in Action!

- "I notice that I got up on time to get ready for school. I did not keep pushing the snooze button and then wait too long to get up making me late for school. I notice I am more calm when I have more time to get ready too."

- "Michael, I know you got angry with Jamad but you did not start a fight with him or start yelling and cursing. By staying in control, you're helping us keep the peace."

- "Even though I wanted to sneak my cell phone into the classroom, I made a choice to keep it in my locker."

Reflect back to the rules you did not break today. Write down at least one:

1. _____

2. _____

3. _____

Reflect on the toll taker and Shamu. Choose to see rules followed and drop the rope as

---

KEY POINTS

Clarity Canon Moments/Proactive Recognitions:

1. **Be clear about rules, boundaries, personal code of conduct and start rules with the word "no".**

2. **Lookout for rules followed and make a point of recognizing yourself and others for following the rules.**

3. **Talk about rules and respecting boundaries when they are being followed.**

4. **Respond to rules broken with a reset—whether it's for someone else or for yourself.**

5. **Move right back into greatness by recognizing the next success.**

---

low as necessary to create success. Move away from reacting to rule-breaking and into Clarity Canon Moments, or proactive recognitions of rules being followed.

Strategy 4: Creative Recognition (Creative Chris) : Creating Success That Would Not Otherwise Exist

Creative Recognition builds on Active Recognition, using clear, simple commands and bigger-than-ordinary positive statements in response to any movement toward rule following. This helps move you closer toward success. This makes success unavoidable and helps us build trust in ourselves and in others. We learn how to notice in ourselves and others the smallest success. We make the ordinary things into extraordinary things. Here is an example on how to apply to yourself:

The Heat is On

Let's say you decided you need to lose weight and learned from your physical education teacher that it is healthy for you walk 10,000 steps per day. You are wearing a pedometer (this counts steps) every day. In the very beginning you are still not 100% committed to doing this but you want to feel better emotionally, help your stress levels and lose weight. Every day you notice that you are being successful even if you only did 3,000 steps. You do not focus on that you did not do the other 7,000 steps. You focus on the steps you did make. Notice that every day you are moving closer to walking 10,000 steps per day.

What is something that you can notice for your baby steps to success?

_____

_____

_____

Let's look at how to notice this in others:

At a meeting that you are leading, Jordan looks anxious and annoyed, as though he has something important he needs to say and is waiting for the right moment to chime in. "Jordan, I see you have something to say, and I need you to wait until I finish speaking." He waits even though you know how hard that it is for him. Then when you are finished with your announcement, ask for his input. Then recognize him: "I could see how hard it was for you to wait to give your feedback. You really are very excited about this project. I like how patient you were and allowed me to finish. Thanks for helping us keep a peaceful and productive meeting."

Keep in mind that you do not focus on the fact that Jordan keeps raising his hand even though the rule is to wait until everyone is done with their portion. Remember no energizing rules when they are being broken. He is in fact not interrupting by raising his hand even if it annoys you. Do not energize your healthy negative emotional response and do not energize his constant hand waving during a meeting.

We can creatively recognize others for putting forth genuine effort, making difficult changes, overcoming obstacles, and staying on a path of personal growth and achievement.

SHAMU TIME: The ropes are all over Shamu's tank, making success impossible to avoid.

You're opening your mind up and looking at what is going strong rather than what is going wrong. **Positivity Points: Creative Chris and Creative Recognitions**

Pay close attention to what you and others are doing. Notice when there is any movement toward following rules and make a statement about those baby steps.

When requests are complied with, bring in Polaroid Power and give Experiential Recognitions: what values or qualities are you showing yourself or do you see in others? Point out greatness qualities—character strengths and virtues. When not making requests, be as creative as possible in seeing opportunities to energize for smart choices. Energize each step that is made in the direction of success.

The Heat is On

Reset Raphael

What if you or someone else is breaking a rule? Raphael Reset is the answer. We practice resetting ourselves and others. Ms. Bravo has a great way of explaining it: Reset. Restore. Restart. Let's look at the meaning of these three words:

Reset:

_____

Restore:

_____

Restart:

_____

Because you are all familiar with modern day technology you have all likely seen a reset button. I am sure that you know what reset means. Here we learn how to reset ourselves and others. When we or someone else gets off track, we simply reset without drama. Some people do not even use the word out loud and others may use a sign. You will find what works for you.

When we restore ourselves, we are applying coping and calming skills to our thoughts and emotions. Perhaps it is a breathing technique, or turning yourself away for a moment or even saying out loud like, "I need to reset myself." Sometimes we need to apply more techniques like the REBT techniques when it is really hard for us to shake it off and we feel really disturbed. Things like this help us shift our attention while we prepare to restart. After taking those two steps we are ready to start over with a new outlook and new response. In other words, it is like a STOP, RELAX, THINK and NOW START OVER technique.

When a rule is broken we do not lecture, remind, warn or explain. When we reset ourselves we do not start with self-doubt or rating ourselves or others. For example, when we reset someone else or a group if someone was gossiping, that person knows full well why they were reset. And if there's any confusion about why the reset happened, you can clear it up as soon as the gossiping stops by shining Polaroid Power on that situation by giving a Proactive Recognition to energize how the no-gossiping rule is being followed. Using the word *reset* gives us a chance to remind ourselves and others that we can reset ourselves away from negativity as soon as we realize it is happening. Think of it as a keyword that supports us in getting rid of an unhealthy negative thought, negative behavior or an unhealthy negative emotion that arises. Think of it like a light switch: we quickly shut off the negativity and turn on the positivity.

When we reset others, we are not scolding them or trying to shame or embarrass them. We are reminding them that they have the power within themselves to get right back on track.

Some people are having fun with the word recalculate, which reminds us of our inner GPS—that part of ourselves that calmly recalculates when we make a wrong turn and guides us back in the right direction. Think about the GPS in a car. Does it scream at you and pull out the rule book if you made a wrong turn?

Practice Resetting Yourself

It is a little challenging to practice reset unless you happen to be breaking a rule in this moment, but know that you are learning about a new technique to help yourself and others to stand for positivity, smart choices and healthy self-control. Although, we do not like to encourage you to think about negative things to come, write down a situation that occurs regularly that you are thinking about using the technique of reset:

_____

_____

_____

REMEMBER: Use reset when someone texts you or says something online about you or someone else that is mean or hurtful. Also remember that by resetting in that way you are also practicing healthy ways to communicate and to resolve conflicts. Sometimes we can easily misread what someone writes online or in a text and if we reset ourselves and ask to speak to them on the phone or in person because you are not clear and do not want to assume the worst, you are showing that you value that relationship with the other person.

The Heat is On

Just like On Demand TV, you can tune into your greatness any chance you get. You can also tune into other's greatness and positivity. How will you work on tuning into your greatness and positivity and the greatness and positivity of others? What is your plan? Go back to the Top Eight to Being Great. These tips will increase positivity and greatness in your life. Pick one daily to work on and practice it until it becomes a natural way of behaving, or being in your life. Below are more strategies to help you:

The 12 Happiness Enhancing Strategies

1. **Counting Your Blessings:** Expressing gratitude for what you have (either privately through contemplation or journaling—or to a close other) or conveying your appreciation to one or more individuals whom you've never properly thanked. (CHAP 4)

2. **Cultivating Optimism:** Keeping a journal in which you imagine and write about the best possible future for yourself, or practicing to look at the bright side of every situation. (CHAP 4)

3. **Avoiding Overthinking and Social Comparison:** Using strategies (such as distraction to cut down on how often you dwell on your problems and compare yourself to others. (CHAP 4)

4. **Practicing Acts of Kindness:** Doing good things for others, whether friends or strangers, either directly or anonymously, either spontaneously or planned. (CHAP 5)

5. **Nurturing Relationships:** Picking a relationship in need of strengthening, and investing time and energy in healing, cultivating, affirming and enjoying it. (CHAP 5)

6. **Doing More Activities that Truly Engage You:** Increasing the number of experiences at home and work in which you "lose" yourself, which are challenging and absorbing. (CHAP 7)

7. **Replaying and Savoring Life's Joys:** Paying close attention, taking delight, and going over life's momentary pleasures and wonders—through thinking, writing, drawing, or sharing with another. (CHAP 7)

8. **Committing to Your Goals:** Picking one, two, or three significant goals that are

meaningful to you and devoting time and effort to pursuing them. (CHAP 8)

9. **Developing Strategies for Coping:** Practicing ways to endure or surmount a recent stress, hardship, or trauma. (CHAP 6)

10. **Learning to Forgive:** Keeping a journal or writing a letter in which you work on letting go of anger and resentment towards one or more individuals who have hurt or wronged you. (CHAP 6)

11. **Practicing Religion and Spirituality:** Becoming more involved in your church, temple, or mosque, or reading and pondering spiritually-themed books. (CHAP 9)

12. **Taking Care of Your Body:** Engaging in physical activity, meditating, and smiling and laughing. (CHAP 9)

From Lyubomirsky, S. The How of Happiness: A Scientific Approach to Getting the Life You Want. New York: Penguin Press www.thehowofhappiness.com

Your Body:
What's Food & Activity
Got to Do with It?

Activity 7.1 — Activity 7.2

Your Body

By Irene Maltzan

What you eat has a tremendous effect on how you feel. Did you ever eat too many cookies or other dessert and at first it tasted good then the next minute you felt tired or you got a belly ache? That was a sugar crash. We don't connect our mood to food but it can have a huge influence on how we feel and most people, including adults, don't get the right education in nutrition. Most people learn proper nutrition and exercise when they are already overweight, told by their doctor or get an adult onset disease such as diabetes.

How do we learn about food? We are born and bottle-fed or breast-fed and then we eat what our parents prepare for us. It's not until most of us move out of the house that we become independent eaters. Until then we eat pretty much like our parents eat. If your parents are knowledgeable about nutrition that is great but the fact is that most people know very little about nutrition and how to prevent obesity. Some are just lucky to be thin or have good genes but the majority of this country is overweight.

The obesity problem is out of hand in this country. The three main causes of disease are still poor nutrition, lack of exercise and smoking. Wow! That hasn't changed in 50 years even though we live in the information age of TV, the internet and social media. We just have too much information and people aren't sure what to believe.

Let's take a look at why you should care. Kids are also affected. The 2012 statistics show that that 16.9% of American kids are obese. That is one in three kids. This has been consistent for the last five years. The good news is that we can all do something about it. We can change what we eat and our habits to become healthy normal weight adults that expect to live a long time. Let's take a look at what causes obesity and poor health. Then we will explore how you can make the changes that will help you be a healthy kid and adult. It's easier than you think. Remember awareness is the key to change.

Let's start with testing your knowledge on sugar and how much of it you have in your diet.

1. How often each day do you drink sugary drinks (i.e. soda, ice tea, juice)?

   a. 2 or more

   b. 1 time a day

   c. Never

2. How often do you eat sweets such as cookies, candy, ice cream a day?

   a. 2 or more

   b. 1

   c. Never or rarely

3. How many teaspoons of sugar are in a soda?

   a. 0

   b. 5 times a day

   c. 10

4. What does eating sugar every day do to my body?

   a. Nothing

   b. Gain weight and have bad skin

   c. Eventually develop adult onset disease and increase chances of obesity

If you answered mostly C's you are in good shape. You have been taught well, live with a nutritionist or have learned to stay away from sugar. Good job.

If you answered mostly B's you are in between. Although you have sugar you don't have it in unlimited qualities. You need to cut down when possible and have it as a treat, not a daily part of your diet.

If you answered mostly A's you need to stop drinking and eating sweet and sugary foods every day. You are damaging your health and eventually it will lead to many health problems that you can avoid. Learning to make better choices is key.

Your Body

Making Changes Now Helps You Later On In Life

Sugar

If you want to be healthy, have energy and avoid adult onset diseases then you need to understand what sugar does to your body. Sugar, especially processed cane sugar and high fructose corn syrup, are the third leading causes of adult onset diseases according to the American Dietary Association. Most people's food pantries contain massive amounts of sugar and they aren't even aware of it. These sugars are in ketchup, barbeque sauce, bread and salad dressing just to name a few things. Almost all processed food, unless it is pure protein, contains some form of sugar. Then our drinks are made up mostly of sugar. The average American consumes 20-50 teaspoons of sugar a day. This is about seven-15 teaspoons per meal. Most people wouldn't eat that much sugar from a sugar bowl but when it is disguised in drinks and all other processed food it's hard to tell what you are eating.

Based on what you just learned write down three changes you would like to do to have less sugar in your diet. An example may be, "I will only drink water during the day" or "I will only have fruit for dessert except on special occasions."

Three specific changes I will make to improve my diet when it comes to lowering my sugar intake are:

1. _____

   _____

2. _____

   _____

3. _____

   _____

Now come back in a week and see how you did. Small changes add up to big results. Even changing one habit at a time will help you be healthier. Next see how you feel making the changes. Once there is less sugar in your diet you will feel more energized and have fewer cravings.

How awesome is that? Healthy food is delicious. Here is a recipe to prove it.

This is an example of how real food is healthy and delicious. Most people that try this recipe can't believe how amazing it tastes and how easy it is to make.

RECIPE: Banana Ice Cream

Peel several bananas and place in freezer until completely frozen. Remove the peels before freezing. After they are frozen break them up into several pieces and throw them in a food processor with a couple of tablespoons of water and blend until they become smooth like ice cream. Transfer to a bowl and enjoy! Don't like bananas? Try mangoes or strawberries instead.

Nutrient Dense Food: Vitamins and Minerals

After looking at sugar now the next step is to see how much nutrient dense food your diet contains.

Nutrient dense, in case you don't know, is how many vitamins and minerals a food has compared to its calories. For this exercise you will need to figure out what type of food you eat each day. To help you understand answer the following multiple choice questions. This is a way for you to learn more about nutrition. There are no wrong answers.

1. How often do you eat vegetables?

    a. 2 or more

    b. 1 time a day

    c. Rarely or when my parents make me

2. How often do you eat fruits?

    a. 2 or more

    b. 1 time a day

    c. 1 time a week or rarely

Your Body

3. When you eat bread or pasta is it white, white with fiber added, or whole grain?

    a. Whole grain

    b. White but it has fiber in it

    c. White with no fiber

4. What kind of protein do you eat?

    a. Chicken, fish and turkey burgers

    b. Red meat, chicken, turkey occasional chicken nuggets or burgers

    c. All kinds, including chicken nuggets, hot dogs, salami and fast food burgers

If you answered mostly A's you are doing really well with your diet. It is important to eat a wide variety of food and the healthy type of protein. Keep up the good work.

If you answered mostly B's you eat fairly well but need to add more fruits, vegetables, fish and leaner proteins to your diet. Try to eat whole grain instead of white flour products with added fiber. Remember that fast food and anything breaded or fried is a treat. Always choose whole grains over white flour products for added nutrition.

If you answered mostly C's you need to cut back on processed food and food that is high in fats and calories. White flour is not healthy. It is stripped of its nutrients and has a lot of calories but not enough nutrients. In addition to sugar most people gain weight from too much processed food, white flour products and not enough fresh food.

Now Eat All Your Vegetables!

To feel good and have lots of energy eating vegetables is really important. Vegetables are the types of nutrient dense foods that our body needs to stay healthy and have good energy. Did you know kale is a nutrient powerhouse! Just one cup of steamed kale contains 1328% RDA Vitamin K and 354% RDA of Vitamin A. Mushrooms are one of the few foods that have Vitamin D in them. That is why they are an important cancer fighting food. Eating onions can help stabilize your blood sugar. Learning about vegetables and their nutritional value can be fun. They add flavor and make your meals interesting. Frozen vegetables are good too. However you can get them in your diet it doesn't matter. Getting three cups of vegetables a day is a great way to stay healthy, lose weight if you need to and have good energy. If you eat them every day they make your skin clear, your eyes bright and your hair shiny.

The healthiest vegetables are the green ones like broccoli, kale, dandelion greens, spinach, collard greens and broccoli rabe. They contain the most macronutrients. Macronutrients help us build muscles and help the muscles recover. They also give us energy. They are called macro because we require a lot of them each day.

Be open to trying one of the green vegetables that are healthiest for you. They can be raw, roasted, sautéed in a pan or steamed. Try to eat one cup a day. This will be the best thing you can do for your body, even better than taking vitamins.

What About Fruit?

How about fruits you may be asking? Yes, fruits are important and healthy. Contrary to what most people believe not all fruits are created equal, just like vegetables aren't all created equal. Some fruits have more health benefits than others. Some fruits are high in sugar so using portion control is really important

Grapes are a good example. A serving of grapes is 12 grapes but most of us can eat two or three times that amount. For the same amount of grapes you can eat twice as many strawberries, blueberries or raspberries. They have more vitamins and fiber and have less sugar. Other fruits that are high in sugar are watermelon, oranges and raisins. Fruits that have a lot of nutrition benefit are apples, pears, plums, berries, melons and peaches.

To make these changes bring your list from above of healthiest fruits and vegetables to the grocery store. Choose two fruits and two vegetables you never tried. Write down the fruit or vegetable and how you liked them.

1. _____

2. _____

3. _____

4. _____

After you tried the new fruits and vegetables repeat this exercise every month and you will increase the amount of nutrient dense food in your diet tremendously. Remember if

Your Body

you didn't like something that is fine too. We can't like everything we try. The important thing to remember is not to give up. The fruit and vegetable family is made of hundreds of varieties. You are bound to like some of them.

Protein

One food group that is most important to have at each meal is protein. The human body needs protein to grow and repair cells. Without adequate protein most people feel sluggish and tired. They may even develop anemia or a lack of iron, which is a constant feeling of fatigue. Too much protein on the other hand, especially the wrong kind, can lead to weight gain and intestinal irritation. It can make your kidneys work overtime and as a result become damaged and this is not good for your health. The right amount of protein to eat at each meal is about the size of your palm.

The Protein Breakfast experiment is an exercise to see how you feel when you eat different types of breakfast. This is really important to do well in school, sports and have good energy.

Protein Breakfast Experiment

Breakfast Day 1 - Eat cereal or oatmeal with milk and a piece of fruit

Write down when you became hungry and how your energy level was. Make a note of how soon you were hungry and how tired you felt.

Hunger level after one hour? _____ Hunger level after two or more hours? _____

Energy level after one hour? _____ Energy level after two or more hours? _____

Breakfast Day 2 - Eat pancakes or French toast with fruit and some syrup

Write down when you became hungry and how your energy level was. Make a note of how soon you were hungry and how tired you felt.

Hunger level after one hour? _____ Hunger level after two or more hours? _____

Energy level after one hour? _____ Energy level after two or more hours? _____

Breakfast Day 3 - Eat scrambled eggs with turkey bacon or sausage

Hunger level after one hour? _____ Hunger level after two or more hours? _____

Energy level after one hour? _____ Energy level after two or more hours? _____

NO Skipping Breakfast—NO! NO! NO!

One mistake that most people make is with breakfast. They either eat no breakfast at all or end up eating too much carbohydrates and sugar at breakfast. If you want to feel your best throughout the day then eat protein for breakfast. Eggs despite the bad rap they got years ago are one of the healthiest forms of protein. Especially if prepared without too much fat. Other good breakfasts are natural peanut or almond butter, grilled cheese on a healthy English muffin or turkey bacon. Overall staying away from eating high sugar breakfast cereal, fruit flavored yogurt, white flour waffles and pancakes with syrup is important to feeling good and maintaining healthy weight.

Why Are Grains so Important?

Let's talk about whole grains and why they are important. In order to understand why whole grains are better for you, first you much understand why white flour isn't good for you. There are several reasons why white flour is unhealthy. White flour is stripped of the most nutrient-rich parts of the grain. It also is processed in a way which makes it instantly absorbed when it reaches the intestine. Whole grains take a much longer time to be digested, absorbed, and broken down into energy while white flour immediately raises your blood sugar levels, much in the same way sugar does. Yes that is right, just like sugar does. That means that after you eat it, your body has two choices: either burn it off immediately, or store it as fat. Unless you are working out while eating your white flour bagel, that means that it is stored as fat. In addition, because of the instant elevation of your blood sugar level, the later instant drop of your blood sugar will likely leave you hungry. It's like being on a rollercoaster with the constant ups and downs.

White flour and sugar are very similar in the ways they affect our energy, bodies and health. Both can be major reasons for weight gain. If your diet is filled with a lot of white flour, you are likely missing out on some major nutrition necessities, and feeling very hungry a lot of the time. It's OK to have a little now and then, but it's much better for your health to eat whole grains instead. If you really find that you cannot control yourself around white flour products then just like someone who can't control themselves with cookies, you might find it easier to cut it out of your diet. You will see a big difference in your health if you do give up white flour and replace it with whole grains.

According to the Whole Grains Council, "Whole grains contain all three parts of the kernel. Refining normally removes the bran and the germ, leaving only the endosperm. **Without the bran and germ, about 25% of a grain's protein is lost, along with at least seventeen key nutrients.** Processors add back some vitamins and minerals to enrich refined grains, so refined products still contribute valuable nutrients. But **whole grains**

are healthier, providing more protein, more fiber and many important vitamins and minerals."

When grocery shopping, look for whole grains that have at least three grams of fiber and the whole grains stamp on it. Marketing can be deceiving by telling you a product has whole grains but remember adding back vitamins and minerals to enriched refined grains isn't the same as a whole grain product. The following is an experiment to see the difference between the two.

Whole Grain Experiment

Take a white flour product such as a hot dog roll or piece of white bread. Shape it into a ball. Keep rolling it until it is small and the shape of a ball. Put it aside. Next take a piece of real whole grain bread such as Ezekiel bread (can be found at health food stores) and try to make that into a ball. It will crumble because it can't be made into a ball. Notice the difference. The white flour product is a big blob of white flour while the whole grain bread resembles a grain. What do you want sitting in your stomach? Now you can really see the difference between a whole grain and a white flour product!! Remember don't be fooled by a label. Only products that are real whole grain can have this label.

Activity 7.1

Drink AT LEAST 64 ounces of Water Per Day

We are made up from 55% to 78% water depending on our body size. Our brain is made up of 70% water. It's important to understand this because depending on how we treat ourselves we can change the energy of the water in our body. Have you ever seen a swamp? Look at a picture of one. It is dark, slimy and it is stagnant. The complete opposite is a river. It is clear; the water is rushing and moving. That is how your body is. Did you ever see an Olympic runner? They have so much energy. How about someone that sits on the couch everyday and watches television? There is a big difference in their energy levels. If you sit still every day and play video games or watch television your body becomes like a swamp. You may have very little energy or feel sluggish all the time. If you get outside or exercise for at least thirty to sixty minutes a day your body becomes more like a rushing river. It will have lots of energy and you feel and think clearly.

The U.S. Food Pyramid used to be the way to teach everyone about nutrition but it has now been updated and renamed ChooseMyPlate.gov. ChooseMyPlate.gov is a much better way of showing us what and how much to eat. We use plates not pyramids when we eat so visually it is easier to understand what and how to eat. Portion control is key. You can be the healthiest eater on the planet but if you eat too much food it can cause weight gain and poor health. By portioning and putting the right amount of protein, fruits and vegetables and whole grains you can have optimal health and weight for your entire life. If we taught this to children from kindergarten there would be less obesity and diseases.

The changes made to MyPlate are easier to see and show the correct portions of food group instead of leaving it up to your imagination as to what a serving looks like. Vegetables are most important and can be eaten in larger quantities than other foods. Protein, fruit and grains are about equal in size. Dairy should be eaten like a condiment instead of as a main course. That means sprinkling parmesan on your pasta or shredding some into a salad would be better than slabs of it on a cheeseburger or nachos.

Being as healthy as you can be at any age is a choice. Once you have the right information to help you understand how nutrition works for you, then you can figure out what's right for you. Learning to eat healthy is not an easy thing to do. It takes being aware of what you do each and every day. It doesn't mean we have to be perfect but if you eat healthy at least 75% to 85% of the time then you will be healthier than ¾ of the rest of the population. Nutrition is not a priority for most people unless they have been raised from an early age to understand it or unfortunately become obese or sick.

Activity 7.1

MyPlate Experiment

Before dinner, take a paper plate and looking at the picture, draw the lines on the paper plate to show the different food groups. Now when you eat dinner compare what you put on your dinner plate to the paper plate to see if you are eating the correct portion amount. If you eat everything and are still hungry you can go back for more of the vegetables. This way you can stay full and be healthy. Most people think they know correct portion sizes but until you actually see it drawn out on a plate you can easily overdo it on protein, grains or dairy.

If you want to be healthy, have good energy and maintain healthy weight understand what natural food is vs. processed food. Eat as much natural food as possible. I like the saying, *If you didn't grow it or kill it don't eat it.* Watch portions and drink lots of water. It's actually really simple. It doesn't require a lot of thought once you understand what good food is and you will feel unbelievable once you eat this way. Only you can make this choice for yourself so make the change to natural food and see how incredible you can look and feel.

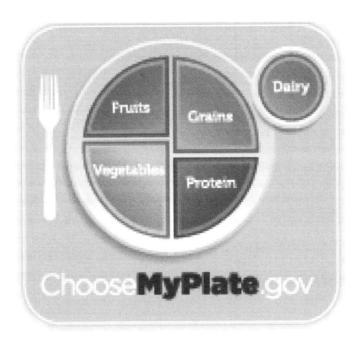

By this time we are sure that you have heard so much on this topic. You may have been part of a DARE program at one point. You may be abusing drugs and alcohol at this moment or may know someone that is and while this is usually a time for some teens to experiment in the world of drugs and alcohol, this is also a time when teens put themselves in very risky and even dangerous situations. Let's look at some facts to keep this fresh in your mind. And if this is you, you need to check yourself and be honest first with yourself if things have gotten out of control.

If you have a parent(s) or grandparent(s) who has struggled with a drug addiction or alcoholism, you are at greater risk for becoming addicted if you continue to abuse drugs and/or alcohol.

- Abusing drugs and alcohol ruins your relationships with family and friends.

- Brain cells are damaged and you jeopardize your ability to make safe and smart decisions.

- Teens who abuse drugs and alcohol frequently begin failing their classes.

- Girls are often at risk for sexual assault in situations where drugs and alcohol are being abused.

- Some teens die by overdosing, suicide or by making unsafe decisions that put them in harm's way.

These are just a few facts. Go to SADD: Students Against Destructive Decisions at **sadd. org/stats.htm**. Select three facts that either surprised you or was something new for you to learn. You can click on any of the categories on that page. Write them down here:

1. _____

2. _____

3. _____

Discuss these as a group if you are working with a group, if not discuss with the adult who is coaching you through these exercises.

What are your thoughts? Write them down:

_____

_____

Activity 7.2

What are your feelings? Are you concerned about yourself, a family member, a friend? What action can you take if you are concerned about yourself or someone else? Remember be honest with yourself. This is your life and you are the leader of your present day situation and your future.

Take Action

Would you consider becoming an advocate? Or organizing a chapter at your school or in your community? Check out this information to show you how: **sadd.org/formchapter.htm** This is a great cause for Tribal Warriors to stand for and you would have a national support network.

Consider perhaps a Contract for Life from the SADD website. Go here **sadd.org/contract.htm** to download the contracts.

So what will you do to help yourself or someone else? Write it down here:

NOTE: There is a great deal of help if you or someone is in trouble. Don't keep this a secret. Don't worry if you "rat" someone out in this situation. They do not have to know it was you if you do not want them to but you are helping them and their parents save their lives.

REMEMBER: Safe, Smart and In Charge. We want you to be safe, make smart decisions and to be in charge of your life!

By BJ Byrd

Isabella is a student in Mrs. BJ's physical education class. She is a bright and bubbly student who is usually friendly and outgoing. Lately Isabella has been showing up late to class, not dressing for class at all and putting forth less effort than usual. Mrs. BJ often sees her standing by herself with her arms wrapped around her waist as if she is trying to hide something.

Finding Isabella's behavior to be changing by the day, Mrs. BJ decides it is time to have a one-on-one conversation with her before class begins. As Isabella approaches her class number for roll call, Mrs. BJ walks towards her and says, "Hello Isabella. It is so great to see you in class today, dressed and ready to participate. I appreciate the fact that you take my class seriously and want to improve your fitness. This tells me that you are interested in leading a healthy lifestyle. I love seeing your smile because it warms my day."

Isabella wraps her arms around her waist and begins to turn her head away from her teacher. Mrs. BJ decides it is time to notch it up a little and says, "I see you wrapping your arms around your waist and turning your head away from me. I want to acknowledge that even though physical fitness may not be your best subject, I am so proud that you showed up for my class dressed today." Isabella responds, "I don't want to be here. I hate my body."

Mrs. BJ in turns says to Isabella, "I hear you say that you don't want to be here and that you hate your body. The fact is that even though you are feeling that way, you still dressed and came out to your number. Only someone who is responsible and courageous could do that. I want to accuse you of being a dedicated student, who takes learning seriously." After a long pause Mrs. BJ tells Isabella, "I know how you feel. When I was a teenager I felt the same way about my body as it was going through all of its changes. I was wondering if you would like to work with me on an individual fitness program. I would be willing to meet with you before school to show you some activities to help you feel better about your body. In fact it would be a privilege to work with you! Are you interested?"

The F.I.T.T. Principle

An easy way to look at fitness is using the F.I.T.T. Principle, which stands for "frequency," "intensity," "type" and "time". Below is a short description of each. For more information searching the internet is a great tool.

Frequency relates to how often a person should workout. For cardiovascular activities (e.g. walking, jogging, biking, etc.) it should be at least three times per week while resistance training such as weight lifting or resistance bands should be three to four times a week.

Activity 7.3

Intensity relates to how hard a person works out. It is important to stress or overload the body so that the muscles begin to adapt, but to not workout so hard that it takes a long time to recover or leads to injury. With respect to cardiovascular training one typically looks at a person's heart rate. This is called the Target Heart Rate. For moderate activity level the target zone is 50%–70% of resting heart rate while vigorous activity is considered to be 70%–85% of resting heart rate (cdc.gov/physicalactivity/everyone/measuring/heartrate.html). For resistance training, intensity is typically related to the number of repetitions (rep) an activity is done and the amount of weight for each rep. The higher the weight or reps, the higher the intensity. Another way to increase intensity is to reduce the amount of rest time in-between each activity.

Type relates to the kind of activity a person completes in order to achieve a particular result. For both cardiovascular and resistance training it is important that the activities are continuous in nature.

Time relates to how long an activity is done. Cardiovascular and resistance training should be done for 30–60 minutes a session.

A key component of any activity program is REST. Rest allows the body to adapt to the workload and then recover. It is a commonly held belief that the harder the workout, the longer the body needs to recover. Another important component of any workout program is to drink water before, during and after any activity as it provides a way for the body to stay hydrated and cleanses your organs and muscles. Keep in mind that it is critical to change your activity routine every 4–6 weeks as your body adapts to the current workload and needs to be challenged by increasing frequency, intensity, type or time. Currently the Center for Disease Control recommends that children/teens get at least 60 minutes of physical activity per day (cdc.gov/physicalactivity/everyone/guidelines/children.html).

For a teen like Isabella, it is important to start off slowly and provide a variety of cardiovascular and muscle building activities. As she builds confidence in herself and her body image, she will discover more enjoyment in exercising. There are many benefits to maintaining a healthy lifestyle including a reduced chance of developing heart disease, diabetes and certain types of cancer; controlling your body weight; increasing your mental health and mood; and strengthening bones and muscles (cdc.gov/physicalactivity/everyone/health/index.html). Easy ways for Isabella or anyone for that matter to increase their cardiovascular fitness is to walk—walk to the store, walk to school, walk your dog… just plain walk (or ride your bike).

Create a challenge on Facebook or at your school, church, synagogue, or temple. Ask everyone to do something for 20–30 minutes per day. Ask them to post about it. Share your ideas for challenges with us by blogging at **tribalwarriorsblog.com**.

By Carly Mentlik

What is yoga? The word yoga means "to unite"—to connect with your true self and feel the connection you have with everything else in the world. It's just what being a Tribal Warrior is all about—tapping into the connection we have with everything, supporting each other, uniting to create change in ourselves and through this inspiring others to change too.

Yoga was developed thousands of years ago in India. It's best known in the United States as a physical practice, which it is. It's also a way of living and offers ideas for learning about yourself. The concepts of yoga are very similar to everything else you've been learning about so far in this workbook. For example, mindfulness, inner wealth, gratitude, unconditional self-acceptance, compassion for others and the world and living from your heart rather than your head.

Why practice yoga? Yoga begins from an idea that everyone gets weighed down by doubt and insecurity because of past negative experiences. This causes feelings of dissatisfaction, separation and affects the body. None of the ways we try to get rid of the bad feelings, like escaping into our minds, comparing ourselves to others, focusing on things we don't have, or numbing ourselves through unhealthy habits ever lasts in helping us feel better. It's just like our friend Justice from the Greatness Academy who is learning to battle with Worrying William, Miserable Marvin and Doubting David. That's why yoga is called a "practice," because since we keep forgetting about our truth, we need to practice every day to help us remember.

All of the work you've done so far has helped you learn many ways you can help clear those negative thoughts from your mind, for example practicing unconditional acceptance of yourself, others and life in general. All the poses, breathing and meditations of yoga help you learn to connect with your body and feel okay with who you are. Yoga gives your warrior self a new tool: a way to move the negative thoughts and feelings out of your body.

Your Body

What Kinds of Things Can Practicing Yoga Help Me With?

There are so many benefits to practicing yoga. Here's a list of some. Once you start to practice, you may realize that it helps you in ways you hadn't even considered and you can add to the list.

- Reduce stress

- Relax, find inner peace

- Balance your moods

- Develop strength, balance and flexibility

- A fun way to exercise and increase energy

- Helps performance in other sports

- Helps concentration in school and work

- Improve communication of how you really feel

- Learn to accept yourself for who are at each moment

- Compassion for yourself and others

- Use your intuition to make decisions

- Resist peer pressure

Is Yoga Really for Me?

You may already have an idea about what yoga is, either from seeing it on TV or in the movies. Sometimes, having preconceived thoughts in your mind about something can prevent you from trying it. So, here are some myths I've heard people share about yoga—the good news is they aren't true. Yoga is for everyone!

Myth: You have to be flexible to practice yoga.

Truth: A lot of people think this because they see pictures of people twisted up into pretzel-like shapes or touching their heads to their toes. Those kinds of poses can be fun to look at, but it's not important at all if you ever have a chance to move your body like that. With yoga, you start where you are and you practice to improve from that point. All that truly matters is the effort you put in. You can create a goal for how you want to improve, but the real goal is to practice accepting yourself for exactly where you're at each day and not letting yourself feel badly about what you can't do. There are people who are paralyzed, who have severe disabilities and people who are over 80-90 years old who practice yoga every day—and they're great at it!

 CAUTION: Make sure to listen to your body and respect its limits. Don't push yourself further than you're ready to go. The yoga poses are all broken down into stages, called kramas. You move up in small steps to make sure that you're building the right foundation before you move on to trying harder poses.

Myth: Yoga is only for girls.

Truth: The truth is that when yoga was first practiced in India, it was actually only allowed to be practiced by boys and men. Women who chose to practice yoga often had to leave their families and societies to do so, because it wasn't considered appropriate. Indra Devi was one of the first known woman yoga teachers. Women weren't typically accepted as yoga students but she kept persisting and finally was allowed to study with Krishnamacharya, one of the most influential teachers of yoga as we know it today. Indra Devi helped spread yoga outside of India and be accepted as a practice for girls too. It may seem like the opposite today because so many females practice yoga and it may seem like males don't. In reality, there are many guys who practice yoga. As only one example, many athletes, both male and female, who snowboard, surf, play football and many other sports are starting to realize how much yoga helps them improve their performance.

Myth: You have to believe in Hinduism and it conflicts with other religious beliefs.

Truth: While it is true that yoga has roots in the Hindu religion, you don't have to believe in it to practice yoga. The ideas are universal and you don't have to explore any part of it that doesn't feel right to you. Whatever you believe in, whatever religion you may practice, whatever cultural beliefs you have, all of those ideas can be incorporated into your practice of yoga. When you meditate you can call upon whatever feels right to you. If you don't believe in a god, practice any religion or aren't quite sure what you believe, that's ok too.

Your Body

Poses and Practices Points

- The physical part of yoga can help you strengthen your whole body and improve your balance and flexibility.

- When you focus your mind on aligning yourself in the poses, it helps to still your other thoughts so you practice being completely in the present moment.

- Yoga poses teach you about yourself: how you react when trying a hard pose, how you feel when you see someone more flexible, if you tense up and hold your breath when you're uncomfortable—it all shows you the kinds of things that take you out of the present moment and into your mind.

- There are many different styles of yoga—if you don't like one, don't assume that yoga isn't for you. Try another style or another teacher and see if you can relate any better.

ACTIVITIES: Visit this link and scroll down to click on the yoga playlist to check out videos to help you get inspired, get started and to see some other people your age who are practicing yoga (**youtube.com/mandalalearning**).

- Watch some of the teen yoga videos for inspiration to get started.

- Try some sun salutations. Choose one or more of the sun salutations videos in the playlist to try. Start with three or more of these in the mornings before a longer practice or other exercise and you will warm up and energize your whole body.

- Try one or more of the other videos that look interesting to you.

Which ones did you like the best? Which ones would you like to go back to and try? Write them down here so you can start to create a list that will be available to you whenever you want to practice.

_____

_____

_____

_____

Activity 7.4

Here are some links for introductions to some of the postures.

- **Yogaminded.com** is a great place to start. This site was created with teens in mind. Under "Yoga 4 Teens" choose "Poses for teens" to explore "12 poses teenagers should know."

- **Yogajournal.com/poses** has pictures of many more poses with detailed explanations. Play around on this site to explore poses by category, body part or click on "therapeutic focus" to find poses to help with things like anxiety, insomnia and stress.

Try some of the poses that look interesting to you.

What are some poses you liked? Write them down here.

_____

_____

_____

_____

What are some poses you'd choose if you wanted to...

Relax?

_____

Energize?

_____

Improve balance?

_____

Your Body

What about some specific body parts you want to focus on, either for to increase strength and flexibility, or ones that are sore and could use a good stretch?

Body Part	Pose Name	Link Where I Found It

Are you really enjoying yourself and want to explore more? Here are some links to sites that have free online classes.

- **Yogisanonymous.com**; click on LIVE and you can choose from lots of free classes, by length of class and level. If you try one and don't like it, try a different teacher or choose a class by a title that sounds cool.

- **Yogajournal.com/video**; there are lots of free classes here and you can choose by length, level, or a specific type of pose or body part to focus on.

Want to practice with other people?

- Invite some friends over to do one of the videos with you.

- Google some local yoga studios and see if they have any classes for teens. If they don't, practice your leadership skills by writing, calling or visiting and ask them to start one. If there are classes and you don't have the money to attend, try asking the studio if they would consider a work exchange for participating. A lot of studios and teachers do this to help people out who want to practice yoga and may not have the extra money to do so.

Breath and Meditation

- Breathing is the simplest and most powerful tool in yoga—anytime you're fully paying attention to your breath, you're in the present moment.

- Paying attention to your breathing helps you concentrate and provides a focus away from the thoughts in your mind.

- Breathing can relax the brain, muscles, nerves and remove old energy from the body.

- Whenever you're doing any of the poses, make sure that you are paying attention to your breath the whole time. You'll notice that if you start using your mind too much, you'll probably be holding your breath.

- Start each movement with an inhale and move through them inhaling, exhaling, inhaling, exhaling…

Getting Started Meditating

Sit comfortably with your back straight and shoulders back, (or start lying down if it's hard for you) close your eyes and pay attention to your breath as you inhale and exhale slowly and deeply. Don't judge yourself if you can't do it for that long before getting lost in your thoughts. Just go right back to paying attention to your breath…inhale, exhale, inhale, exhale, inhale, exhale…it may also help to use one of the breathing exercises below and/or use a mantra, because it gives your mind something to focus on other than your thoughts.

Breathing Exercises

There are many types of breathing techniques that can help you increase different energetic states in your body, for example, some work for calming you down and some help your blood flow easier and energize you. Here are some types of breathing and benefits. After you decide which type may be best for you at this moment, you can follow the links below to read about them and watch how to do them.

Diaphragmatic Breathing: Many people don't breath with their diaphragm and may not even know what it is. Learning how to breathe through your diaphragm can help reduce stress, bring more oxygen to your cells and also protect your back when you move.

Ujjayi Breath: This is sometimes called "ocean breath" because you constrict the back of your throat to make an ocean sound. It can also sound like you're fake snoring. The ujjayi

Your Body

breath can help you drown out your thoughts and focus your mind on the movement and who you are outside of your thoughts.

Nadi Shodhana (alternate nostril breathing): Can help you bring balance to your body.

Kapalbhati (fire breath): Can increase the oxygen in your body, energize and heat up the body.

Links:

- Visit yoga journal for breathing exercises, instructions, benefits and suggestions of poses to do. Visit the "yoga breathing exercises" playlist at **youtube.com/mandalalearning** to watch video clips of these different types of breathing.

- To read about the benefits of diaphragmatic breathing and how to do it, go to **stress-management-for-peak-performance.com/diaphragmatic-breathing.html**.

- Check out this online breathing room. Look at the online guided meditations where you can choose different themes, kinds of breath, colored backgrounds and the time.

Which breathing exercises do you think would be the most helpful for you to incorporate into your life? Why?

_____

_____

_____

Which ones are you most likely to do on a regular basis?

_____

_____

_____

Mantras

Using mantras in your yoga practice and throughout your day can also help you drown out negative thoughts and stay focused on more positive emotions and thoughts. The word mantra means "mind tool." You may already do this naturally, if you ever repeat something to yourself over and over to help you remember it, like "I can do this, I can do this."

To create new mantras, think about some feeling or state of being you want to bring into your life and work it down to a short phrase or sentence. Whenever your mind starts to wander, or some negative thoughts creep up, you can replace them with your mantras.

Some examples:

- I am calm

- I surrender

- I am strong

- I am here

- I accept myself for who I am

M.Y.O.M (Make Your Own Mantras):

1. _____

_____

2. _____

_____

3. _____

_____

Ideas for Living Yoga

Start a Journal Keeping a journal can be one of the most powerful ways of learning about yourself. If you commit to reflecting about yourself and your relationships each day you can learn about your patterns, see how you change over time and can practice putting your thoughts and feelings into words. You can write, type, draw, video yourself, make a voice journal—do whatever feels right and you'll enjoy doing it often.

Some journal questions to get you started:

- What obstacles are there in your life that get in the way of you being yourself? Of finding inner peace? Of finding passion and motivation?

Activity 7.4

- What can these obstacles teach you? (For example, to be stronger, to stick up for yourself, etc.)

- What are some things in your life that help you overcome these obstacles or forget about them?

- What are some changes you can make in yourself and your life right now to bring you more peace? How can you change your thoughts? Your actions?

Make Playlists Make some music playlists for different moods and kinds of yoga practices you like to do.

- Make some for times you want to relax, some for when you want more energy.

- Explore themed playlists, like "patience" or "strength".

Write On Your Mirror Use dry-erase markers to write quotes, reminders, inspiring words, etc. on the mirror in your bedroom or bathroom. You see the space all the time and it's easy to change the writing whenever you want.

Create Your Own Altars Creating a personal altar can be a fun, creative way to connect with certain feelings and energy, things you want in your life and things you want to remember. A common assumption about altars is that they're only associated with religious ceremonies. Yet, people have used altars across cultures since prehistoric times, to bring comfort, luck, to remember ancestors and all kinds of other reasons. You probably already have some form of an altar, whether it's a collection of pictures, a group of memories from a trip or a magazine collage. Alters can be any size, any materials, at home, for travel—use your intuition and explore your creativity!

Practice Seva-Seva Seva-Seva is a yoga concept that means "selfless service." It's simple, but not always easy: do something helpful for someone or something without expecting anything in return—no reward, or even recognition. It can be anything from listening to a friend or smiling at someone who helps you at a store, to volunteering for a cause you care about—t hey all contribute to creating positive change.

Make These Deposits Daily

Activity 8.1 — Activity 8.3

Make These Deposits Daily

> "Self-discipline begins with the mastery of your thoughts.
> If you don't control what you think, you can't control what you do.
> Simply, self-discipline enables you to think first and act afterward."
>
> —*Napoleon Hill*

With freedom comes responsibility. If you want to have more freedom, you need to show your parents, caregivers and other adults that you will make choices that keep you safe, smart and in charge. Take control of your life. Don't let others control you or push your buttons.

The information that you are learning is information that when put into practice helps you to make smart choices, and stay safe and in healthy control of your life at home, school and in your playtime with friends. Remember to think about this easy to remember slogan, *Safe, Smart and In Charge*. When challenged with a an opportunity to choose right from wrong, think about your safety, is it wise and am I in control?

ACTIVITY: Create a billboard, collage, iMovie, YouTube video, poem, rap, song lyrics or whatever you wish that calls attention to being Safe, Smart and In Charge.

Write down what it means to you to be safe:

_____

_____

_____

What are smart choices? Write down three:

1. _____

_____

2. _____

_____

3. _____

_____

What does it mean to you to be in charge or in control of your life?

_____

_____

_____

Write down the strengths, values and positive qualities that the above answers reveal. Name at least three:

_____

_____

_____

Be Responsible for The Energy You Bring Into Any Space

All of our thoughts and behaviors is energy. All life is energy. Think about the energy that is transmitted through an iPod or radio. You are transmitting energy all over the place. What kind of energy do you want to bring around with you and transmit out to the world?

_____

_____

_____

What kind of energy do you want to be around?

_____

_____

_____

You have most likely heard the expression "What comes around goes around" or "You reap what you sow." What do you want to come back around? Positivity or negativity? Healthy and fun relationships or unhealthy and hurtful relationships?

_____

_____

Make These Deposits Daily

Be the change you want to see and be responsible for the energy you bring into any space at home or school, or during your downtime with friends.

Namaste

In India, they use a meaningful and powerful way to honor one another and it is called Namaste, which is an ancient Sanskrit word. In getting back to our roots in a tribal sense, think about us as one. We honor by recognizing with verbal or virtual Nurtured Heart® techniques but taking it a step further to learn something from another beautiful culture we can practice Namaste which is like a slight bow of the head with hands pressed together held close to your chest near your heart.

When you use this gesture, you are saluting or recognizing someone else's presence or existence in society and universe. The greeting means we are united and there is complete acceptance. It also recognizes equality between us. We honor the sacred fact that we are interconnected. When using this gesture you are saying non-verbally, "The spirit in me greets the spirit in you, I bow to the divine in you."

In that spirit, we are taking this journey into Section Two and coming together in a powerful way to change the world. We began with you and you are on your way to transforming. NOW it is time to change the world and we are starting with your homes, schools and communities.

SECTION TWO:

Tribal Warriors Stand Against Violence, Hate Crimes & Bullying in Schools & Communities. Tribal Warriors STAND for Positivity, Respect & Compassion Toward Themselves & Others

Introduction

Now that you have completed Section One and your Inner Wealth has increased, you have learned how to apply the lessons to your own life and how to relate better with your family, friends, team and class mates. Continuing with flourishing and changing your life for the better, Section Two pulls you closer together as a tribe, the human tribe to stand against all types of bullying, hate crimes and violence in your schools and communities. It is the belief that before we can address bullying to increase peaceful relationships, we need to build up all individuals, whether they have been the victims or the bullies. We believe that all teenagers need the information presented in this workbook in order to stand together to build peaceful Nurtured Heart® communities.

Leadership:
We Are All Leaders

Activity 9.1

Leadership

We are calling upon you to develop a social and cultural movement to stand for peaceful school and home environments, peaceful virtual communication and rock solid peaceful personal relationships. You do not have to be an offender or victim to learn the important lessons in this section. We all need to understand that we are a collective, a tribe, and what affects one person affects us all as human beings. If one person is abused, bullied, sexually assaulted or killed, than we have all been violated. Many times the people who do the bullying and who act abusively have learned how to be that way and they need these teachings to help them learn new ways of being. Similarly the victims of abuse and bullying may have been victims of abuse in their families and they need this information to learn how to empower and protect themselves. Research has taught us that victims have higher rates of being victimized more than once. Interestingly, we have worked with many teens and some end up in abusive relationships even though they come from very loving families and they are blind-sided, or completely taken off guard. You will all learn what healthy and unhealthy relationships are, which is at the mezzo level (meaning small groups) and one-on-one interactions at the micro level.

A warrior is much more than someone who learns to gain power over others through combat or warfare. The intense energy of warriorship can be used for peaceful purposes. Dr. Shamita Das DasGupta, an expert in family and domestic violence, reminds us that we can create peace by encouraging forgiveness. In her extensive work in both India and the United States against acts of violence, she reminds us that forgiveness is used as a powerful action or stance that was taken by leaders like Dr. Martin Luther King, Gandhi, Mandela, TuTu and many others. It was used as a positive act of resistance and challenge. As Dr. Shamita Das DasGupta say, "Forgiveness must be connected to courage and not weakness."

Select one of the leaders mentioned above. Who did you select?

_____

What did you learn about them and forgiveness or peace?

_____

_____

_____

In learning the Nurtured Heart Approach®, we download new software to make this change. We learn techniques that enable us to practice speaking a language of nonviolence and positivity. Your major role as a leader is to be relentless and fearless with implementing this new style in your life. Keep resetting yourself into this new and healing way of communicating and relating to others. Set the example. People will get used to it—whether they like it or love it!

Think about the fact that you are the leader of your life or your future. Every day when you choose to wake up on time for school and get yourself ready, you are making a leadership decision. Leadership has to start with you first—in your heart and in your mind. When you take ownership of your life and make smart choices between what is right and wrong or good and bad, you are making a difference in your world and in the lives of everyone you touch at home, at school and in the community.

Once you start showing strong leadership for your personal well-being, you will also then become a good role model for leading other people. At this point, we need to select the five person Tribal Warriors Leadership Team, or the guiding coalition to join forces for a good cause and that is about you, your family, your school and communities. Keep in mind if you are learning this individually or learning this as a group, everyone needs to learn and practice what these team members represent. Here is a refresher from the introduction:

The Tribal Warriors is comprised of Kool Kodak, Polaroid Power, Clarity Canon, Creative Chris and Raphael Reset. In any school year the gender can change for any leadership role. Clarity Canon, Creative Chris and Raphael Reset are always Senior Leaders. Because their responsibilities are a bit more sophisticated than the others they need to have leadership skills that embrace all the leadership techniques we are learning here and they need to deliver their share with perseverance and precision in a more notched up way.

Leadership

Raphael Reset
Kool Kodak
Clarity Canon
Polaroid Power
Creative Chris

Kool Kodak delivers Active Recognitions. He notices everything that's going right. Whomever he speaks to comes away feeling special. Even if it's something small—a choice to follow the rules, or handling strong feelings, or just showing up and paying attention—he has something good to say about it. Practically everywhere he goes, Kool Kodak takes "snapshots" of successes, both miniscule and massive, and he's unfailingly generous when giving feedback to team members about those successes. Another way to think about Kool is to imagine that you hold a mirror up in front of someone and just describe what you see. You are not being fake, just making real observations. The "kool" news is that you can even apply this technique to someone that you do not know or maybe that you do not even like so much, you know those annoying students or maybe one of your brothers and sisters who get on your last nerve. This technique helps you communicate with others in a real way instead of ignoring or perhaps arguing with someone.

Polaroid Power amps up the Active Recognitions with Experiential Recognitions. Polaroid comes in with a zoom lens and really lays it on thick. As a more seasoned student, she can keep up with Kool Kodak in terms of noticing and acknowledging success. Like a Polaroid camera, she captures successes as they happen, then deepens that image of success by clearly stating how those successes reveal strengths and virtues. Her unique, intense style takes some getting used to, but in the end, this ability to hone in on what's going right—and on what's so right about it—makes her an invaluable leader of the team.

Clarity Canon can clearly see when rules are not being broken and she delivers Proactive Recognitions. Clarity is the team's ultimate school policy implementer and relentless rule follower, but she's not one to lecture, reprimand, or scold when rules are broken. Instead she recognizes *rule-following*. She keeps students in full compliance by offering frequent reminders to those staying on task: *you are wonderful for not breaking rules and* *for following policy.* Clarity Canon appreciates fellow students for their willingness to change old habits, for staying in healthy control and for re-routing themselves back to compliance when they break rules or fail to comply with school policies and procedures. She's firm and strict, but also compassionate, loving, and proactive.

Creative Chris believes in giving Creative Recognitions. Creative believes that you are flourishing for the slightest movement toward success and smart choices. His view is that giving recognition for every success, brilliance, and accomplishment is good for everyone, including the one who gives that recognition. He notices what his fellow students are doing in the moment—or even what they're wearing!—and takes the time to tell them what he's observing. He communicates to the other students that he values them for their positive attitude and great work ethic. He is the one most likely to get so creative that he could sound like his other team leaders but there is something unique about him and his technique. Even when students seem to be having a rough day, he finds ways to positively acknowledge them for their ability to deal with hard times or difficult tasks. The really interesting thing about Creative Chris is that he has this ability to notice even the slightest movement toward positive change and he jumps on it. It is like he has superpowers for seeing these things. It's like he has a hawk eye for that detailed, minute movement and then he swoops in and notices it publicly! Creative Chris is especially magnificent at bringing students back to balance when necessary. Indeed he is often the one who is able to de-escalate crises at the school and his team members enhance on what he does. While he doesn't always hit the mark, he responds to his own errors and negative thoughts by redirecting his focus to what's great and right in the moment.

Raphael Reset is the one that helps us get right back on track. He believes that a rule broken is a rule broken. A little bit of hurting yourself or others, is hurting yourself or others. If he sees anyone arguing, he comes right in and resets them back to their great qualities and peaceful communication. He is pretty cool because sometimes you do not even know you have been reset. His technique is very powerful because he teaches us about healing and feeling better quickly by staying on track and working to achieve any goal we set. Raphael Reset does not allow us to make things worse by feeding negative thoughts or behaviors, even for a second!

The big trick with all of these ways to show radical appreciation is to eventually learn how to radically appreciate and recognize your strengths. Focus on what is going strong rather than what is going wrong. And notice it about yourself. Students who make it to these leadership roles are without question students who have awesome "inner wealth" and that is because they have managed to apply these techniques to themselves despite any of their backgrounds, labels or any hard times they have experienced in their childhood and teen years.

Leadership

How will you decide who will be on the leadership team at your school or program? Will you vote? Ask people to volunteer? Select someone who you know already is a great role model? Write down some ideas for a plan here:

_____

_____

_____

_____

_____

REMEMBER: you do not have to use the funny names that you are reading about. Your unique and beautiful names are already the best names. You can of course choose to have some fun with those names or the symbols from the patch but that is up to you and your group. The important thing is to apply the techniques that they represent, they are our recognitions: Active (Kodak Moments), Experiential (Polaroid Moments), Proactive (Canon Moments) and Creative, as well as one Reset technique, and the three stands and the four concepts: Shamu, Toll Taker view, video game and sports game models. If you already are thinking who would be great role models for these leadership roles, write them down here and discuss as group:

_____

_____

_____

"To survive the lessons ahead, you're going to need
far more energy than ever before," Socrates warned him that night.
"You must cleanse your body of tension, free your mind of stagnant
knowledge, and open your heart to the energy of true emotion."

—Dan Millman, From Way of the Peaceful Warrior

Here is another refresher from the beginning of this book. What are we standing for and against? This tribe holds to the principles of the following three stands. In other words this is what they fight for in warrior-like fashion:

> **Stand One: Refuse to Energize Negativity ("Absolutely NO!")**

> **Stand Two: Relentlessly Energize the Positive ("Absolutely YES!")**
> Fiercely recognize what is going strong rather than what is going wrong.
> Create success and positivity any chance you get.

> **Stand Three: Clearly and Unenergetically Enforce Limits (Absolute Clarity)**
> Set up clear limits and stick to strict consequences when those rules are broken.
> Maintain personal boundaries with a clear code of conduct.

CREATIVITY TIME: Create posters, blogs, iMovies, or YouTube videos about these three stands. Learn them inside out, upside down, backwards and forwards. These three stands support the strength of the recognitions. Each one holds equal weight and is equally important just like all of you. No one is more important or less important than the other.

By sticking together as a tribe we can extinguish negativity in our personal lives, with our friends, in our families and in our schools and communities. United we stand, divided we fall is a very popular motto used by many nations and states and has been used in songs. Think about it in this way, unless people are united, it is easy to destroy them. When people come together to take a stand, a powerful force of unity is created. A warrior can be described as a person who is brave and courageous. A warrior has strong intensity of action and effects change. She is strong-minded and cares for her body. He is well balanced and keeps his mind and heart open to learning and changing but never forgets he is part of a tribe. A warrior is fierce, assertive and energetically ready to take a stand at any given moment.

GROUP ASSIGNMENT: Find out what you can about Warrior Gods and Goddesses, or tribal warriors. Do your own Googling and then come back together to discuss what you find. What strengths are in warriors? Why are they called warriors? What did they stand for and protect?

_____

_____

_____

Universal Human Rights

Activity 9.2

Universal Human Rights

"Where, after all, do universal human rights begin? In small places, close to home—so close and so small that they cannot be seen on any maps of the world. Yet they are the world of the individual person; the neighborhood he lives in; the school or college she attends; the factory, farm, or office where he works. Such are the places where every man, woman and child seeks equal justice, equal opportunity, equal dignity without discrimination. Unless these rights have meaning there, they have little meaning anywhere. Without concerted citizen action to uphold them close to home, we shall look in vain for progress in the larger world."

—*Eleanor Roosevelt*

ACTIVITY: Look up Universal Human Rights. Have a discussion on this quote and the meaning of human rights.

Taking Stands for Social Justice

Dr. Shamita Das Dasgupta shares her knowledge as both an activist and advocate regarding the work Rev. Desmond Tutu, Nobel Peace Prize recipient in 1974 and first black South African Archbishop.

His prescription as components of social justice is as follows:

1. **Public/overt recognition of the harm done to someone/group;**

2. **Making amends for the harm done, as much as possible; and**

3. **Changing the social conditions that allowed the harm to take place**

In Nurtured Heart® terms, we refuse to look the other way. We proactively recognize ourselves and others when we see that harm is NOT being imposed. We shout it out loud. Additionally we work to forgive ourselves for looking the other way and we practice compassion toward ourselves and others.

> "We lose ourselves when we compromise the very ideals
> that we fight to defend. And we honor those ideals by
> upholding them not when it's easy, but when it is hard."
>
> —*President Barack Obama, Nobel Lecture, December 10, 2009*

Heart-centered leaders in huge corporations create values that guide all their decisions. Imagine that you are a CEO (Chief Executive Officer). The truth is you are the CEO of your personal business and that business is your life. In Section One we created your own personal boundaries, or values that you are standing for. In Section Two we need to create values for the way we treat each other and the values we want for our schools and communities.

Here are the ones we suggest. You can add to them or change them. With peace, perseverance and hard work we will not fail to reach our goals. We are committed to creating a peaceful environment at home, school and in our communities.

- **We communicate openly and move toward solutions.**

- **We honor and respect one another.**

- **We care about each and every person with whom we are in contact and their safety is of the utmost importance.**

- **We are aware that oppression exists and believe in equal treatment regardless of race, gender, sexual orientation, religion, age or cultural ethnicity. Everyone's voice holds value.**

- **We treat everyone with dignity and respect.**

ACTIVITY: Spend some time discussing these values and decide which ones you want to keep. Together create a poster for your school or organization.

Values: What Do We Stand For?

Activity 9.3   Activity 9.4

Values

When you think about other teens in your school how do you think about or see them? Do you notice their hair, skin color, the way they dress, behave or speak?

_____

_____

_____

You will likely say yes to that question because quite honestly, you have been taught this and sometimes if you thought about it and responded in a healthy and accepting way, this is completely okay. The issue with seeing people like this is that often times it comes with judgment of others. Start noticing when you meet someone how you view them. Let's start with thinking about someone you know that seems different than you.

Who are you thinking about? _____

What did you notice he/she is wearing? _____

_____

Is their skin color different than your skin color? _____

Does that make you curious about them if it is different? _____

Do they dress differently than you? In what way? _____

_____

As you can tell there are many questions that we can go on endlessly about.

- **Do you think of people as weirdos, geeks, jocks, gangstas, etc.?**

- **Do you use terms that address someone's sexual activity? For example we often call boys or men players or gigolos but if a girl is with more than one boy she is called vulgar names and is marked "easy."**

- **Do you value others more highly if they wear designer clothing? Do you judge others if they dress in cultural clothing? Does this mean they are better or worse off than you?**

- **Do they practice a different religion than you?**

- **Do you judge others because of who they are attracted to?**

- **Are people who study a great deal "nerdy" or geeks?**

- **Do you put people down if they do not seem as smart or are smarter than you?**

When we accept others unconditionally, we accept them for their unique greatness. We accept that people make mistakes as well. When people treat us unfairly we know that we can handle it without reacting to it or rating them. When we accept others in this way, as hard as it really is, we are able to handle unfairness in the world. We can all make choices as to how we treat others and some people choose not to be fair and can be pretty vicious. We know this. We just need to learn how not to give them energy and then channel our strong feelings to make change in the world and in some instances to help us deal with insanity! We also need to cease and desist, meaning STOP RIGHT NOW to treat others unfairly in our thoughts and actions. The change needs to start from within us.

Cultural Knowledge: Jain Tribes as a Model for a Path of Non-Violence

> "The Jain religion, an Indian religion, is founded on active nonviolence. This religion is part of our ancient wisdom dating back to 9th century B.C. As a Jain, one has to promise to practice nonviolence in words, thoughts, and action."
>
> —*Dr. Shamita Das Dasgupta*

ACTIVITY: What will you do beginning right now in this moment to practice a path of non-violence? What harmful words, thoughts or actions can you work on ridding yourself of to live a path of non-violence?

_____

_____

_____

Strive to be a "Jina," which is a conqueror or victor and is someone who has conquered their inner enemies. By building your personal inner wealth, you become a "Jina."

NOTCH IT UP: Notice what you are doing and what good character you are showing by perhaps being honest or being real. What does that say about you?

Values

Active Recognitions (Kool Kodak) and Cultural Diversity

Instead of giving a usual hello to someone, practice using an Active Recognition, which can be quite meaningful in a person's life. Active Recognition powerfully states that you value that person for who he or she is in that moment. Many times some teens can feel invisible in schools and communities. Active Recognition turns this energy upside down, proving that no one is invisible—that they are seen and even celebrated each time they walk through the door.

Active Recognitions are also great for igniting conversations that can lead to conversations about culture. When done without judgment as a respectful recognition of difference, this shows genuine interest and can open up a conversation where you both can learn from each other. This helps us understand each other and builds good relationships, which then leads to better communities.

Here are some examples you can use to learn more about the beautiful differences among us:

- **To a friend or someone you do not know who brings a traditional Indian dish from home for lunch: "Rajinder, I see you've brought food from home for lunch today. It smells so different from the way my family cooks, can you tell me about it?" Keep in mind that you do not have to like the smell of the food. Be real. Our palate or our sense of taste and smell often needs time to adapt to new flavors. The point is that by noticing the difference as compared to what you would eat in your home, you are recognizing the difference in culture and by recognizing that you are honoring that person and their culture.**

- **To a Muslim teenager who wears a traditional head covering to work: "Sarwat, that's such a colorful head scarf. I would like to learn more about the reason women and girls who are Muslim have to cover their heads."**

Write down some ideas of your own on how you will actively recognize someone that is different than you:

_____

_____

_____

Don't feel shy if the difference is about skin color or even an accent. When you use an Active Recognition respectfully and share with that person that you would like to learn more about them and their culture, be real. Be yourself. You could even tell them you want to learn more about other cultures.

REMEMBER: By accepting, appreciating and recognizing culture and other greatness qualities, we are installing positive emotions and by doing that, we are breaking down the walls that divide us and tearing down oppression hopefully in a bulldozer style. Remember we become more of "we" versus "me" when we do that. The tribe is more important than the individual.

Values

When you hear the word "peace" what is the first thing that comes to your mind?

_____

_____

_____

The word peace sometimes brings to mind its opposite: war and violence. The absence of these things, we think, is peace. But peace is more than the absence of violence: it is about harmony and balance. It is something to create proactively—meaning taking action to create peace in advance instead of waiting to create peace after violence and conflicts occurred.

Cultural Word of Peace

The words shalom (Hebrew) and aloha (Hawaiian) both translate to mean "peace," and they are used as greetings and farewells. In its depth, shalom conveys wishes for safety, good welfare, prosperity, security, fortune, and friendliness. On a personal level, it describes a nonviolent lifestyle that embraces respect, justice, and goodwill. All major religions and many cultural practices within tribal communities have teachings of peace. Remember Namaste and noticing that we have a shared spirit and it is more powerful when we are in that place together as one.

ACTIVITY: Google Time. Wordle time. See how many words mean "peace" in as many languages you can find. Create a Wordle on **wordle.net**. Save it and post to the **tribalwarriorsblog.com**.

ACTIVITY: Tap into your creativity. Write a poem, a rap or lyrics for what peace means to you or what it looks like or what words represent it. If you are artistic, draw it. Create a collage, an iMovie, a YouTube video, or a poster. Remember to submit it to the blog at **tribalwarriorsblog.com**.

When we create a space, any space—whether at home, in school or in our communities—that is one of peace, we are creating a space free from hostility, violence and negativity. But we are also exploring opportunities to create new, healthy relationships and to heal existing relationships that have been harmed by oppression and ignorance.

Let's define "oppression" and discuss as a group:

_____

_____

_____

Ignorance:

_____

_____

_____

What memories do you have of yourself, a family member, a movie actor or someone at school being oppressed by the way someone else is treating them?

_____

_____

_____

What did you do about it? It is okay if you say nothing. Be honest. In the future, we are asking for you to take action but it is common for people not to take action. By being honest, you will help others to realize this about themselves. You too are helping make change in the world. If you did do something, share that with us here and on the blog. We want to hear from you one way or the other. Blog the story: **tribalwarriorsblog.com**.

What Do We Stand Against?

Activity 10.1   Activity 10.4

Activity 10.2   Activity 10.5

Activity 10.3   Activity 10.6

What Do We Stand Against?

"I have a dream that my four little children will one day
live in a nation where they will not be judged by the color
of their skin, but by the content of their character."

—*Martin Luther King, Jr.*

"If you are trying to transform a brutalized society into one
where people can live in dignity and hope, you begin with the
empowering of the most powerless. You build from the ground up."

—*Adrienne Rich*

In the bigger picture, the absence or loss of peace can be traced back to many social/ cultural factors and stereotypes: political unrest, domination, oppression, economic inequalities, glass ceilings, racism, sexism, ageism, homophobia, and religious radicalism. How can our minds and hearts not be affected by these violent, divisive political and social constructs? Until we become aware and committed to making that change that begins with each individual, we will fail to make a difference not only at school or in our communities but within our own lives.

In this section we are going to define and discuss the "'ism's" and phobias that destruct us as a human tribe. Let's Google, define and discuss:

Racism: _____

Sexism: _____

Homophobia: _____

Compulsory Heterosexuality: _____

Xenophobia: _____

Ageism: _____

Religious Radicalism: _____

Socioeconomic Status as an 'ism: _____

Mental Illness Stigmatism: _____

Physically Disabled as an 'ism: _____

Stereotypes: _____

Mentally Challenged as an 'ism: _____

ACTIVITY: Select an "'ism" or phobia that seems to bother you the most. Talk it out. What is bothering you? What change can you make to work against that "'ism?" Sometimes the first step is admitting that oppression exists, still exists and acknowledging the work that needs to be done to cleanse our worlds of oppression and the destruction and negativity that comes with it.

NURTURE YOUR HEART: Take a moment to honor yourself for all you are learning in this moment. Notice how you are paying attention, perhaps asking questions and being curious.

Write it down here:

_____

_____

_____

Blog it at: www.tribalwarriorsblog.com

What Do We Stand Against?

CAUTION: If you or anyone you know is a victim of abuse, help is available. Tell an adult that you trust or call 1-800-799-SAFE (7233).

Because you are a pre-teen or a teenager, we are going to use family violence which is a broader definition than domestic violence because you or someone you know may be affected by domestic violence. Dr. Shamita Das Dasgupta defines domestic violence as a pattern of abusive behavior (e.g. physical hitting, slapping, etc., emotional and verbal derogation, economic control, or sexually forcing someone to do something) toward another person by someone in his or her family, including a spouse.

Family violence is broader in that it includes if a child or an elder is being abused in anyway. The best way to teach this is to introduce you to the concept of Power and Control. Keep in mind that although this wheel indicates that the man is the batterer, there are some instances when a woman is the abuser in an intimate relationship even though it is less common. However, there is an extremely higher percentage of men that abuse and murder women.

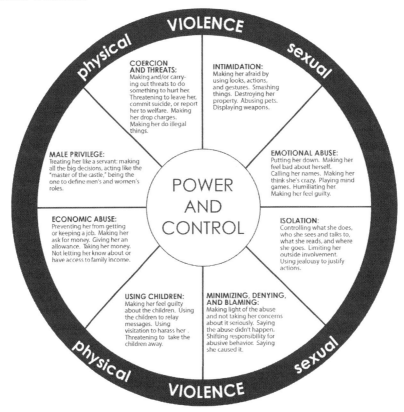

Google Time

Domestic Violence:

_____

_____

_____

Family Violence:

_____

_____

_____

Name a Nurtured Heart® "greatness thing" that you are doing right now in this moment:

_____

_____

_____

What Do We Stand Against?

You may think of violence as a strong word and after learning about domestic and family violence may be surprised that violence has a broader definition. It is important that you understand these concepts because a little bit of violence is violence. A little bit of someone trying to control what you wear, who you go out with or how you think is abusive and is violence. It also is oppressive. Quite often young people confuse this type abuse with "love." Stalking, jealousy, and controlling behavior is abuse.

Google the word "oppression":

_____

_____

Let's review the Power and Control Wheels for teen relationships. (National Center on Domestic and Sexual Violence, **ncdsv.org**)

Compare the equality wheel with the power and control wheel. Discuss in your group or with the person you are working with.

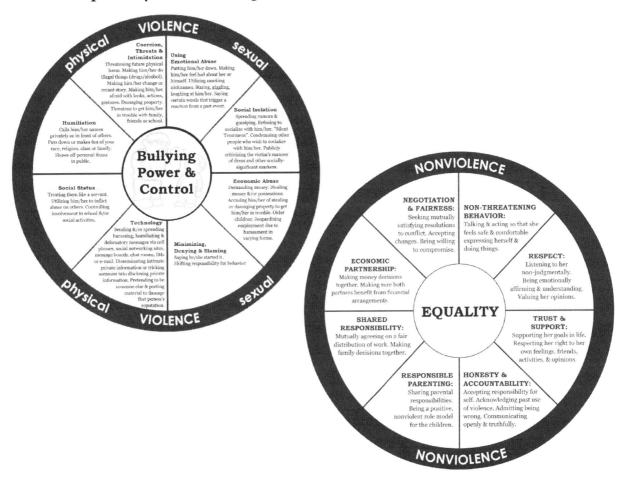

Take a WARRIOR Stance

STAND: We do not energize negativity. That does not mean we ignore it. Reset works to reset yourself or others.

Refuse to allow, accept or ignore any kind of violence you see at home, at school, on the internet or in your community.

 CAUTION: NEVER put yourself in harm's way. Call for help and tell an adult. In extreme situations like physical violence, use of weapons, or people under the influence of drugs or alcohol, call 911.

NURTURED HEART® ACTIVITY: It is not easy to stand for justice. Notice that just learning this new idea that is asking you to take action for the great cause of peaceful relationships says something pretty powerful about your character. Even if you were someone who was not peaceful in the past, in this moment you are not that person any longer. Your past does not define who you are today. Notice yourself. Think about it. What qualities are you revealing to yourself and to others?

_____

_____

_____

What Do We Stand Against?

The word "gang" may enter your thoughts when you think about street and community violence. Sadly, violent gangs in our part of the world in New Jersey and in any other part of the world do not stand for anything other than power and control over a territory or each other. Basically the power and control wheel for bullying applies to the violence we see on the streets that are destroying many beautiful communities where people are afraid to leave their homes and have become prisoners in their own homes. Unfortunately this infection of negativity has poisoned many communities and often, members of gangs are commonly human beings trying to fit in and may be victims of troubled homes or past abuse and violence in their lives. They are labeled offenders, perpetrators or bullies. Their labels come from their less than positive, or bad choices. It does not mean they are bad people. They unfortunately are acting out with bad behavior. We need to find ways to speak to their hearts from our hearts and help them make more positive choices. We need to shout out about their greatness. Here is one way that is exactly what we do when we use the Nurtured Heart Approach®'s Active and Experiential Recognitions. In this way, the entire tribe participates:

Within the Babemba tribe in South Africa, anti-social or criminal behavior is infrequent, but when it does occur, the tribe has an interesting ritual for dealing with it. If a member of the tribe acts irresponsibly, he is placed in the center of the village.

Work stops and every man, woman and child gather around the accused, forming a large circle. Then, one at a time, each individual, including the children, call out all the good things the person in the center has done in his lifetime.

> All his positive attributes, good deeds, strengths and kind acts are recited carefully and at length. No one is permitted to tell an untruth, to exaggerate or to be facetious. The ceremony often lasts for several days and doesn't stop until everyone is drained of every positive comment he or she can muster about the person within the circle. Not a word of criticism about him or his irresponsible, anti-social behavior is permitted. At the end, the tribal circle breaks up, a joyous celebration begins, and the person is welcomed back into the tribe.

—From Sower's Seeds of Encouragement –
Fifth Planting by Brian Cavanaugh

Rational Thinking Activity: Unconditional Acceptance of Others (UAO)

Go back to the lesson on UAO. Reach deep down into your minds and even deeper into your hearts and think about someone you know who is involved with making bad choices at school or in the community. What can you do to remind that person of their greatness? What can you do to accept them unconditionally as a human being first who has made mistakes?

 CAUTION: It is not recommended that you do this if someone has hurt you personally in any violent and abusive way. However if you choose that person, speak to an adult to assist you with the process. Safety is the number one priority which includes your emotional as well as your physical safety.

REMEMBER: Take a Tribal Warrior stance with Stand Two: Create success and greatness any chance you get.

> "Compassion isn't just about feeling the pain of others;
> it's about bringing them in toward yourself."
>
> —*Gregory Boyle, Tattoos on the Heart*

Jamie Gregory, LICS, Advanced Trainer for the Nurtured Heart Approach® suggests an "Activity in Opening the Heart with Compassion."

Focus on the breath. Place your hand over your heart. Sense the heart rhythm. First let's practice with someone you have affection for, a friend or family member. Think about having empathy or sympathy for that person as it relates to something they are challenged with in their lives. By doing so, this creates heart rhythm unity and increases beta waves in our brains. It "instantly" creates that greater empathy space.

Google the word "compassion":

_____

_____

How can you practice compassion? What is your action step?

_____

_____

Activity 10.4

What is kinship?

_____

_____

What does it mean to bring someone "in toward yourself"?

_____

_____

_____

What does it mean to bring someone into your heart?

_____

_____

_____

Practice the act of compassion with Nurtured Heart® Active and Experiential Recognitions. Every time you are thinking about or doing something that is compassionate, notice it. Every time you see someone being compassionate, notice it and shout out about the greatness of being compassionate.

Take a moment and reflect back to a time when you noticed yourself or someone else being compassionate. Share your story:

_____

_____

_____

_____

New Jersey has the toughest anti-bullying laws in the United States. The information below is directly quoted from the New Jersey Coalition for Bullying Awareness and Prevention.

Hazing

Hazing is a form of bullying: it has the two defining characteristics—negative acts by peers and imbalance of power. The problem is that hazing is not acknowledged or recognized as bullying, even by national leaders of the anti-hazing movement, which does such great and passionate work on the issue. The specific problem with not identifying hazing as bullying is two-fold:

1. It leads to underestimation of the prevalence of bullying, when bullying phenomena is not recognized as such; and

2. What we know about bullying and how to prevent and address it is not applied to the problem of hazing. There are two items to access below. One of the items ("key points") is a draft. It needs further review, but it was reviewed and then distributed at a training conducted by NJ Interscholastic Athletics Association this week, and considered helpful by them (an authoritative opinion), so it is being made available here now. The other item ("myths") is an excellent handout accessed at stophazing.org, a major U.S. website for hazing information.

What Do We Stand Against?

NJ Coalition for Bullying Awareness and Prevention

Key Points About Hazing (rev.10/04)

1. Hazing is bullying (imbalance of power, negative acts): What we know about bullying applies to hazing, most important of which is that hazing is caused by adult modeling of hazing and inadequately addressing it when it occurs.

2. Hazing isn't voluntary for participants (isolation isn't an option for youth).

3. Hazing is often seniority-based: When those hazing lacked seniority, they were hazed; most of those hazed later hazed others.

4. Hazing peaks later than bullying (bullying peaks in middle school, hazing peaks in high school, and perhaps later).

5. Hazing always has an organizational setting: it occurs in peer organizations (teams,gangs, fraternities/sororities, clubs, cults, etc.)

6. Hazing youth often acquire their "power" from adults: Adults delegate authority, sometimes by their absence. (Most youth organizations, including gangs, have adult leaders, supporters or mentors).

7. In social organizations, the group's "mission" (and society's interest in it, and expectations for it) obscures hazing or makes it acceptable (e.g., victory for a team).

8. Addressing hazing requires prioritizing non-violence and other values over the mission (the organization needs a "larger purpose").

9. Hazing more commonly than bullying leads to serious injury and death.

10. Alcohol is often a factor in hazing.

11. Adult involvement and supervision (locker rooms, buses, retreats) is especially critical in preventing hazing.

12. Accept discipline, report abuse. (Hank Nuwer, stophazing.org)

Myths and Facts About Hazing

(from stophazing.org accessed 10-29-04)

Myth #1: Hazing is a problem for fraternities and sororities primarily.

Fact: Hazing is a societal problem. Hazing incidents have been frequently documented in the military, athletic teams, marching bands, religious cults, professional schools and other types of clubs and/or organizations. Reports of hazing activities in high schools are on the rise.

Myth #2: Hazing is no more than foolish pranks that sometimes go awry.

Fact: Hazing is an act of power and control over others—it is victimization. Hazing is premeditated and NOT accidental. Hazing is abusive, degrading and often life-threatening.

Myth #3: As long as there's no malicious intent, a little hazing is O.K.

Fact: Even if there's no malicious "intent" safety may still be a factor in traditional hazing activities that are considered to be "all in good fun." For example, serious accidents have occurred during scavenger hunts and kidnapping trips. Besides, what purpose do such activities serve in promoting the growth and development of group team members?

Myth #4: Hazing is an effective way to teach respect and develop discipline.

Fact: First of all, respect must be EARNED—not taught. Victims of hazing rarely report having respect for those who have hazed them. Just like other forms of victimization, hazing breeds mistrust, apathy and alienation.

Myth #5: If someone agrees to participate in an activity, it can't be considered hazing.

Fact: In states that have laws against hazing consent of the victim can't be used as a defense in a civil suit. This is because even if someone agrees to participate in a potentially hazardous action it may not be true consent when considering the peer pressure and desire to belong to the group.

Myth #6: It's difficult to determine whether or not a certain activity is hazing—it's such a gray area sometimes.

Fact: It's not difficult to decide if an activity is hazing if you use common sense and ask yourself the following questions:

Activity 10.5

Make the following inquiries of each activity to determine whether or not it is hazing.

1. Is alcohol involved?

2. Will active/current members of the group refuse to participate with the new members who don't do exactly what they're being asked to do?

3. Does the activity risk emotional or physical abuse?

4. Is there risk of injury or a question of safety?

5. Do you have any reservation describing the activity to your parents, to a professor or University official?

6. Would you object to the activity being photographed for the school newspaper or filmed by the local TV news crew?

If the answer to any of these questions is "yes," the activity is probably hazing.

Adapted from Death By Hazing Sigma Alpha Epsilon. 1988. (Myths About Hazing, from stophazing.org)

"1. If you have to ask if it's hazing, it is. 2. If in doubt, call your advisor/coach/national office. If you won't pick up the phone, you have your answer. Don't B.S. yourself.' 3. If you haze, you have low self-esteem. 4. If you allow hazing to occur, you are a 'hazing enabler.' 5. Failure to stop hazing will result in death..." —Will Keim, PhD, "The Power of Caring"

Distributed by NJ Coalition for Bullying Awareness and Prevention

For information: njbullying.org or (908) 522-2581

> Keep your thoughts positive because your thoughts become your words.
> Keep your words positive because your words become your behavior.
> Keep your behavior positive because your behavior becomes your habits.
> Keep your habits positive because your habits become your values.
> Keep your values positive because your values become your desti*ny*.
>
> —*Mahatma Gandhi*

Activity One: Read and Discuss

How to Unmask the Internet's Vilest Characters

By Emily Bazelon

In June 2009, Lani (a nickname) got a Facebook message from a stranger alerting her to nude photos of herself that had been posted on a website called Private Voyeur—along with her name, her workplace and the city she lives in. The post, titled "Jap Slut," was published anonymously by someone who used a proper noun followed by numbers as an internet handle.

Lani went to the police. She suspected that the poster was an ex-boyfriend who, she says, threatened to kill himself if she didn't pose for naked photographs toward the end of their abusive relationship. According to Lani, when the police questioned her ex-boyfriend, he said that he had distributed the photos among his friends but that he wasn't the one who put them on the web. The police then told Lani they couldn't help her, so she contacted Private Voyeur, which agreed to take the post down. A few months later, though, a new post appeared, with the same photographs and the same information identifying her.

You might think that the legal system offers an easy solution to problems like these—but it doesn't. According to free-speech advocates, there's a good reason for that: Stopping trolls, which is the term used for those who abuse the privilege of the web's anonymous open mike, would mean choking off other critics, which obviously has undemocratic implications. After all, anonymity is a trusted tool of dissidents and whistle-blowers.

Congress and the courts have largely heeded this argument, too. Section 230 of the 1996 Communications Decency Act—the law that matters most for speech on the web—holds that online service providers aren't responsible for offensive content if they've tried to block a little of it. In other words, if you edit some of the comments on your site, you're

What Do We Stand Against?

not liable for the one with a harmful lie that you didn't edit, as a newspaper would be if it published a libelous letter to the editor.

This is fair enough: websites with open comments aren't really like newspapers. But in interpreting Section 230, federal appeals courts went a step further. They have said that the law gives the providers and sites a free pass for essentially all content that users post. That's why Private Voyeur didn't have to police its pages for the reappearance of Lani's photos. It's also why Google doesn't get in trouble for surfacing these posts in search results, which is perhaps even more damaging.

There's no question that the Web would be a more civilized place if Congress changed Section 230 to hold online service providers and websites liable for posts like "Jap Slut" (or Google liable for indexing them) if they have clear notice about what's wrong with the content and still disseminate it. That's how copyright law works online. What's tricky about extending this approach is that some posts would be deleted not because they actually defame or violate privacy but because someone *complains* that they do. The heckler's veto, as it's called, is anathema to free-speech advocates, as well as to the big internet companies, which don't want to be responsible for any user content, given the web's volume and pace. So don't look for Section 230 to change any time soon.

And that leaves people like Lani in a lousy situation. Their only option for using the law to punish trolls is to sue for defamation or invasion of privacy, as Lani has done. The problem is that while she could win a court order unmasking the troll's identity (and ultimately win damages), it's hard to bring such a suit without making her own humiliation complete. Though the "Jap Slut" post and pictures are public, they're still largely out of sight. Lani's children and parents don't know about them, and neither do the customers at her business. But if she were to file this kind of suit, Lani would risk linking the photos to her name forever, not just in the web's dark corners but also in court documents and news coverage.

Which is why we need to pursue another way to take legal action—one that has been out of favor but ought to be given new life in the internet age. We should encourage more anonymous-plaintiff lawsuits.

Fighting an anonymous smear with an anonymous lawsuit is a counterintuitive idea—and a lot of judges, including the judge on Lani's case, are reluctant to try it. But there's some precedent in American law for suing anonymously when a case revolves around private sexual or medical facts. That's how we got Roe v. Wade. "These kinds of suits don't squelch much speech, but they still address the harm," points out the University of Maryland law professor Danielle Citron, an expert on the topic. Indeed, if more people sued anonymously, the trolls might understand that hiding behind an online handle doesn't mean you can't be traced—and there might be fewer hateful posts as a result. Courts have ordered Google to turn over I.P. addresses in a few of these cases. The lawyers who represent Lani have two other clients who succeeded in suing their trolls anonymously, and who won settlements while remaining unknown to the public (though not to the defendant) throughout. The lawyers are starting a nonprofit, Without My Consent, to help bring more such cases.

Of course, anonymous lawsuits come at a cost, given the public's legitimate interest in knowing all the facts of a case. That's why courts generally apply a balancing test, weighing the plaintiff's right to privacy against the constitutionally protected presumption of openness in court. But the internet puts a thumb on the scale for the plaintiff, as the U.S. Court of Appeals for the 11th Circuit recognized in a smart recent ruling involving another kind of troll: the Girls Gone Wild video franchise.

The plaintiffs—B., J., S. and V.—wanted to sue Joe Francis, founder of Girls Gone Wild, for emotional distress because they'd been filmed flashing their breasts or having sex when they were too young to legally consent. (Francis and his company have paid millions of dollars in fines for doing this repeatedly; Francis also went to jail on related criminal charges.) These four women said that if they had to bring the case or testify under their own names, they would risk becoming, "internet sensations permanently identified with the videos." As the 11th Circuit noted in granting the plaintiffs' request to sue anonymously, another woman who sued Girls Gone Wild under her own name has been permanently tagged by name as a "breast-flasher" on the highly trafficked Internet Movie Database.

After a trial in April, an all-woman jury agreed that Francis's behavior was "atrocious and utterly intolerable." But they said the plaintiffs hadn't shown he intentionally caused them emotional distress. The women were not awarded money damages. At the same time, their names, amazingly, were never in the press. This seems right. The law shouldn't guarantee victory. But it should let you fight the trolls without doing their shaming work for them.

What Do We Stand Against?

Activity Two: Read and Discuss

From The New York Times
August 18, 2010

Thwarting an Online Bully

By Riva Richmond

TODAY'S bullies are not restricted to cafeterias, gym class and schoolyards. With technology, they can appear in every digital corner of a modern child's life. But parents and children can take heart. Technology can also be harnessed to combat online bullies.

"It's being used to spread the pain, but the positive thing is it can be used to stop the pain," said Hemanshu Nigam, founder of SSP Blue, a security and privacy advisory firm, and former chief security officer for the News Corporation's online properties, including MySpace. Many tools can help you find and remove hurtful content, stop abusive contact and, increasingly, tackle wayward conduct, he said.

Here are tips on how to find those tools and learn how to use them.

MONITOR SOCIAL NETWORKS The most damaging bullying happens on social networks, because the attacks are public.

Bullies can leave cruel comments on profiles in Facebook, MySpace or Formspring, a nine-month-old question-and-answer service embraced by teenagers and used to level anonymous attacks. Bullies can post unflattering photos or videos and create fake profiles or online groups dedicated to bashing people they dislike. There have even been instances of bullies obtaining passwords to the accounts of their targets, hijacking profiles and posting scurrilous comments.

In 2008, a Florida eighth-grader who shared her MySpace password with a onetime friend discovered, after a falling out, that it was being used to post offensive sexual content. Three 14-year-old boys in Newburyport, Mass., were arrested this year after they created a fake Facebook page to harass a classmate. A Seattle middle school suspended 28 students for online bullying of a classmate earlier this year.

The most popular social networking sites are prepared to handle trouble. All these sites let users remove comments from their own profiles and report other content for removal by the site itself. You can also restrict access to a profile using privacy settings, sever friend connections and block and report egregious abusers, who can get kicked off the site.

"It's a constant battle to make sure teens are safe," said Joe Sullivan, Facebook's chief security officer. When harassment appears, "we want to get it down quickly," he said, and typically do it in less than 24 hours.

To report or take a bully off your friends list on Facebook, go to his or her profile and click "Report/Block this Person" or "Remove from Friends." Blow the whistle on hateful content on group and fan pages by clicking "Report Page" and specifying the offense, which helps Facebook prioritize serious incidents. People in photos can dissociate themselves by clicking on the photo and on "remove tag" beside their name. If nudity or other Facebook violations are involved, report it and Facebook may take it down. Otherwise, you'll have to ask whoever posted it to remove it.

On MySpace, you can block an abuser from the abused person's profile page and report him or her by clicking "Contact MySpace" at the bottom of any page. MySpace also allows people to preapprove all comments made on their profiles. Go to settings, select "Spam" and then "Require approval before comments are posted."

If you are staring down a mean comment or question on Formspring, don't answer it, and it won't be seen by anyone else. You can also block the author from contacting you again. To report harassment, click "Help" on any page and submit a complaint. Consider adjusting the privacy settings so only people you approve can follow you, and to block anonymous questions.

BLOCK MEAN MESSAGES Bullies also use e-mail and other message services to spread torment. Nasty messages can be forwarded many times to many people, and are nearly impossible to stop. Although messaging is not quite as public as social networks, it can still be damaging.

But like social sites, web-based e-mail services popular with teenagers generally have codes of conduct that forbid harassment and intimidation, and mechanisms for reporting bad behavior.

In Hotmail, click "Options" at the top right of any page, navigate to "Blocked Senders" and add the e-mail addresses of bullies. In Gmail, set up a filter for offending addresses from the "More actions" drop-down menu and choose to automatically delete future messages (and perhaps also forward them to a parent).

Instant messages typically come from people only after a user has added them to a chat list, and abusers are usually easy to remove, block and report.

Blocking unwanted cellphone calls and text messages, however, requires visiting your carrier's website, gaining access to the family account with a password and then supplying problem phone numbers. It cannot be done from the device itself. This means children

What Do We Stand Against?

who have their own phones and who have not confided in their parents about bullying cannot take action on their own, Mr. Nigam said.

Jack McArtney, manager of advertising and content standards at Verizon Wireless, said the company gave parents control in part because mobile devices were harder to supervise than home computers. He notes that parents are free to share account control with their children. Verizon's Usage Controls and AT&T's Smart Limits for Wireless both cost $5 a month.

BECOME A HALL MONITOR There are several software programs and online services that can help parents detect and address bullying.

Parental-control software, which is installed on PCs your children use, comes in free and paid versions from a variety of companies and involves various levels of intrusiveness. Norton Online Family, a free service from the security software maker Symantec, for example, can monitor social network usage and oversee certain chat lists and I.M. conversations.

SafetyWeb and SocialShield are newer services that can also help monitor social network use. Both charge $10 a month. SafetyWeb finds online accounts tied to children's e-mail addresses and monitors public online activity for signs of trouble—and semipublic activity if, for example, a child is friends with a parent on Facebook. The company is opposed to "spying," said its co-founder, Geoffrey Arone, so it focuses on alerting parents to potential problems by watching for profanity and red-flag keywords.

Recently, SafetyWeb introduced a feature to help parents ask sites to remove abusive content, in addition to assistance it provides by phone.

SocialShield delves deeper into private social network content by having children add its Facebook, MySpace and Twitter applications. With this access, SocialShield monitors and distills what is happening for parents and alerts them to suspect content. It also provides step-by-step advice on handling bullying incidents, said Arad Rostampour, the company's co-founder.

Several new services monitor text messages on smartphones, including Kid Phone Advocate from Parents Are Listening Services and CellSafety from WebSafety (both $10 a month). Both products watch for words and phrases that may be trouble.

CALL THE AUTHORITIES In serious situations, you may need help from your school or the police, especially if there are threats of violence. This means you will need evidence.

Demonstrate the problem with screenshots or saved copies of web pages (choose "save as" in your web browser) and copies of e-mail messages, instant messages and texts. Preserve it yourself, or use software like CyberBully Alert ($14.95 a year) to help you.

For court, it is best to have digital evidence directly from online services and the bully's own computer, said Mark D. Rasch, who formerly prosecuted computer crimes in the United States Justice Department and is now a principal with the consulting firm Secure IT Experts.

Online services do not keep data forever and hard drives get wiped. The easiest and best way to preserve evidence is to enlist law enforcement. Otherwise, you will need a lawyer, a civil suit and subpoenas—and deep pockets.

"Don't wait," Mr. Rasch said. "If there's any credible threat of injury or damage, you want to take this seriously and have it investigated."

Go to this page and print out the document from Common Sense Media on Cyber Bullying. njbullying.org/documents/cyberbullyingpaper.pdf

Discuss this as a group or with the person working with you in this workbook.

What Does Violence Do to Us Inside?

Activity 11.1   Activity 11.2

Activity 11.1

CAUTION: If you or anyone you know is experiencing these issues, we recommend professional help immediately. Go to an adult to help you deal with these issues and to free you from the suffering you are experiencing.

When people are abused, traumatized or victimized by violence, it can be extremely harmful to our minds and bodies. It is also not easy to change our thoughts from irrational to rational or to replace positive thoughts with negative thoughts. It takes practice and then more practice. It also takes a good support team including a therapist.

In the field of psychology and psychiatry where we study the mind and human behavior in many different ways, we have a decent understanding of what happens to us when we experience trauma, violence and abuse. Because of severe situations, our thoughts can become more irrational, our healthy negative emotions can turn into unhealthy negative emotions and then we get involved with self-defeating behaviors. We reviewed this in Section One when Rational Emotive Behavior Therapy (REBT) was introduced in Rational Thinking.

There are a number of disorders and behaviors that can be the result of being victimized, traumatized or abused. Let's explore some definitions together. Let's use **webster.com** or **wikipedia.com** for our definitions. If you are in a group, each person can select a term to look up. If you are doing this independently, start a Word Document and copy and paste the terms onto that document.

Here are the terms we are going to discuss after you find the definitions:

- **Post-Traumatic Stress Disorder (PTSD)**

- **Adjustment Disorder**

- **Depression**

- **Generalized Anxiety**

- **Homicide**

- **Suicide**

- **Substance Abuse**

- **Social Anxiety**

Activity 11.2

Watch the movie "Cyberbully" an ABC Family Original Movie.

After watching the movie and learning the definitions, connect the dots.

- What did you see happening as it relates to the main character in the movie?

- What negative behaviors did you see in the others?

- What supportive behaviors did you see from family and friends?

VIDEO SUGGESTION: Go to **youtube.com** and look up Amanda Todd. Watch the video and have a discussion about your reactions to these videos.

If there were Tribal Warriors in Amanda Todd's school, what could they have done to stand up for her?

_____

_____

_____

What support did Amanda need other than other students standing for her?

_____

_____

_____

What are your feelings and thoughts about this tragedy?

_____

_____

_____

Creating Inner Wealth
Schools & Communities

Activity 12.1   Activity 12.3

Activity 12.2   Activity 12.4

Activity 12.1

We can all learn together not only how to help ourselves individually but as a tribe. There is some very powerful research that teaches us there can be significant healing and growth after a traumatic event. Acts of violence, including all forms of bullying and abuse are traumatic events to us personally but also to our schools and communities. By this time, you have all likely heard about the students who have opened fire and shot, injured and killed their classmates. An entire community is affected by an incident like this and the healing process can be a very long and hard road but a very possible one.

Positive psychology guru, Dr. Martin Seligman discovered with his group of researchers that people who experienced extreme distress that resulted in PTSD, depression and anxiety, showed higher rates of psychological functioning. The past does not have to define who you are today whether as individuals or communities, or tribes. We have the ability to bounce back, to be resilient. This also does not mean that we celebrate trauma and wish for it to make us stronger psychologically but it means there is **hope**. It means that once we are able to overcome the depression, anxiety and post-traumatic stress symptoms we are physically and psychologically stronger. 97% people are aware of PTSD but far fewer people, about 10% know about Post Traumatic Growth. This can be self-fulfilling in a negative way if something traumatic happens and you believe it will be hopeless because you will develop PTSD. The truth is a large number of people have a normal response of resilience and growth. We too can bounce back and grow together using our strengths to build healthier and more positive environments.

Light the torch of greatness within your heart and pass it on to others. Create a global nurtured heart-warming where we come together as human beings first. Keep the torch lit by taking a stand, taking action and by advocating for peace and positivity.

We can make a change together by taking action. We become activists and advocates. Activists seek to create positive change in the world.

Who comes to mind as someone you personally know or a famous activist you learned about?

_____

List their greatness:

_____

_____

Advocates and activists are often thought to be similar but they are different. An example of activism is when Sojourner Truth delivered her speech, "Ain't I a Woman?," to stand up for her right to vote as a black woman while white women were also fighting for the right to vote. She was brave, bold, powerful and inspirational.

An advocate is someone, or a group, or tribe who speaks on behalf of another group or person. For example if you took a stand and spoke out against bullying of homosexual teens but you are a heterosexual teen, you would be advocate. Or if you spoke about anti-bullying but never bullied or was bullied, you would be an advocate.

Do you see yourself in either role or both?

_____

If yes, what would you do?

_____

_____

Google "Delete Digital Drama" and discuss what you find. How can you make a stand to delete digital drama in your life?

Check out this other website to Stomp Out Bullying. stompoutbullying.org/

Creating Inner Wealth

Here are some things you can do. Check out randomactsofkindness.org/.
This is a good model to learn from. Let's get creative.

What Random Act of Kindness will you do or did you do today?

_____

_____

_____

Go out and RAG on someone: Random Acts of Greatness.

Share one now. RAG on yourself or someone else:

_____

_____

_____

Be a Champion for Compassionate Living. Practice compassion when interacting with others. When you are compassionate you are conscious about another person's challenges or distress and you genuinely want to help them to stop suffering. You can help them by listening and guiding them to others who may be trained to help them but listening, respecting and just being supportive is a great first step.

Do a Gratitude Activity. Appreciate the little things in life that are all around you. Appreciate them in yourself and in others. The Three Greatness Things (TGTs) we learned in Section One can also be the Three Gratitude Things that we are thankful for daily. List three things for which you are grateful for now in this moment:

1. _____

2. _____

3. _____

Create a Positivity Pulse anywhere and everywhere. Remember to be responsible for the energy you bring to any space or place. What is your plan of action to create a positivity pulse in your life?

_____

_____

Shout Out for Peaceful Relationships. Every time you notice people interacting in a healthy and peaceful manner, shout it out. Be sure to shout out virtually on social media sites or send a text.

Encourage your school to do Greatness Shout Outs throughout the day in the classrooms and over the speaker system.

Activity 12.4

Shout Out for Peaceful Relationships and Victories Against Violence. Every time you notice people interacting in a healthy and peaceful manner, shout it out.

Encourage your school to do Greatness Shout Outs throughout the day in the classrooms and over the speaker system. Go on Facebook or other social media forums and be sure you shout out people for being kind and compassionate. Notice when you see NON-VIOLENCE and peace. Take a stand against any kind of violence and support your tribe members when you see them doing it! Go to tribalwarriorsblog. com and report your *victories against violence!* Let's call them our VAVs: Victories Against Violence!

About the Author

Sherry A. Blair

As founder/CEO of her own company, Sherry Blair inspires and motivates others by applying and encouraging positivity. She uses her skills to teach others how to build effective teams, and use non-violent communication to achieve results and resolve conflict. Teaching others to speak from their hearts is a key constituent of the work she does. She is committed to creating and nurturing a positive work environment that allows her team of committed professionals to serve children and families in the state of New Jersey's Wraparound System of Care in their homes and communities.

She is a graduate of Rutgers University with a Bachelor of Arts in Psychology and Women's Studies. She went on to obtain her Master of Science in Social Work with a concentration in Policy Analysis and International Social Welfare as a graduate of Columbia University. Additionally she is dually mastered in Industrial and Organizational Psychology and holds her PhD in Management. Sherry's areas of expertise are providing organizational consulting, coaching, behavioral health services, training and education. She assists organizations with performance enhancement, management coaching, team cohesiveness and effective communication.

Sherry is a New Jersey Licensed Clinical Social Worker, a Board Certified Professional Counselor and holds Diplomate Status as a Professional Coach through the International Association of Behavior Medicine and Psychological Counseling. She teaches Human Behavior in the Social Environment part-time for the University of Southern California, Graduate School of Social Work Virtual Academic Center. Sherry is an Advanced Trainer/Certified Nurtured Heart® Specialist currently serving on the Global Summit Committee for Howard Glasser and the Nurtured Heart Approach®, a transformational approach that changes lives.

For information on how to receive training from Sherry Blair in the Nurtured Heart Approach® and how to utilize our books in your schools, programs or at home, visit our website at **www.isisnj.us** or email us at **info@isisnj.us**. (ISIS Innovative Specialists Inspirational Services, LLC)

To become an Advanced Trainer in the Nurtured Heart Approach®, go to the Children's Success Foundation at **www.childrenssuccessfoundation.org**.

The Facilitator's guide is available on **amazon.com** and where books are sold. To request bulk rates, contact us at **info@isisnj.us**.

Resource/References

Resource Article For Reference

Students Behave Better with Healthy Lunches - ABC News

When a natural foods company made big changes to the school lunchroom at Appleton Central High School in Wisconsin, something radical also seemed to happen among a student body at risk for dropping out.

The soda-filled vending machines at the alternative education high school were replaced with new ones offering only juice, water and energy drinks. Natural Ovens and Bakery, a local company in Appleton, Wisconsin took over the cafeteria and offered fresh fruit and vegetables, whole grain breads and entrees free of additives and chemicals, instead of pizza and fries.

Long standard-issue cafeteria tables made way for round tables, creating a more relaxed feel in the lunchroom. But the biggest change of all was that discipline statistics plummeted.

"I can say without hesitation that it's changed my job as a principal," said LuAnn Coenen. "Since we've started this program, I have had zero weapons on campus, zero expulsions from the school, zero premature deaths or suicides, zero drugs or alcohol on campus. Those are major statistics."

And in classrooms, teachers suddenly felt like they were getting through. "Since the introduction of the food program, I have noticed an enormous difference in the behavior of my students in the classroom," said teacher Mary Bruyette. "They're on task, they are attentive. They can concentrate for longer periods of time."

What Lunch Hour?

While teachers couldn't say that junk food and soda had caused the problems that led the students to be sent to the alternative school in the first place, they did say that the improved school lunches—first introduced five years ago—have made a vast difference in reducing behavior problems.

These aren't statistics that surprise Karen Stout, an associate professor of education at Lehigh University, who has studied more than 2,000 lunchrooms across the United States.

"Atmosphere in the lunchroom carries into the afternoon atmosphere in classrooms," she said. "So that when it's chaotic and fast and hurried, teens come back to class as wound [up], not relaxed and ready to do meaningful academic work."

Medical organizations have banned together and are asking schools to make changes. Their suggestions: longer lunch periods, shorter lines, improved facilities and more adults eating with the students.

Lunch hour is often a misnomer. The average school schedule allows less than 20 minutes for lunch, and there could be as many as 300 teens waiting in line to eat high-fat favorites, like pizza, tacos, and fries.

"Healthier food is better for you," said one student Cayla Schueler who attends Appleton West, another school in the district. "But sometimes you have to just go for the grease."

At a time when childhood obesity is skyrocketing, schools are under attack for contributing to the problem. According to the Department of Agriculture, 76% of schools offer soft drinks while 63% serve salty snacks and high-fat treats

Students Concentrate Better

Students say that food does have an impact on their behavior. "I'd say being able to concentrate better," one Appleton High student, Taylor, said. "Not as tired. More energy."

Another student, Meagan, said that if students went back to drinking soda and eating junk food, the school's atmosphere would change, too. "It would probably be crazy," she said. "People would be bouncing off the walls."

But several schools have recognized that more than a child's health is on the line, and that a better lunch may spell better grades.

Melrose Elementary School in Tampa, Florida transformed their cafeteria into the "Melrose Diner." The school painted murals on the walls, set the tables with tablecloths and flowers and added a sound-activated stop light.

The stoplight changes when the noise in the cafeteria goes above acceptable levels. These days the light is rarely red and the calm in the lunchroom has spilled over into the classroom.

"Boys and girls, the light's on yellow, watch your voice level," the stoplight warned.

Susan Graham, Melrose's principal, said discipline referrals in the last three years have decreased 50%. "Now with this kind of ambience and atmosphere our parent involvement is up 30%," she said.

"We get a lot more done, I think it's a lot more efficient work environment for all of us," Graham said. "We have happier students and happier teachers and much happier principals."

References

Bernard, Michael. (2008). Albert Ellis and the World of Children. Paper presented as part of the symposium "Albert Ellis: A tribute to the grandfather of cognitive behaviour therapy" presented at the 43rd Annual Conference of the Australian Psychological Society, Hobart, Tasmania, September, 2008.

Blair, Sherry. (2011). *The Positivity Pulse: Transforming Your Workplace.* Createspace/ Amazon: Seattle: WA.

Blanchard, K. & Hodges, P. (2003). *The Servant Leader Transforming Your Heart, Head, Hands & Habits.* Nashville, TN: J. Countryman/Thomas Nelson, Inc.

Blum, Robert W. & Libbey, Heather P. (2004). *School Connectedness – Strengthening Health and Education Outcomes for Teenagers.* Journal of School Health, Vol. 74, No. 7.

Boyle, Gregory. (2010). *Tattoos on the Heart: The Power of Boundless Compassion.* Free Press: New York, NY.

Czitchzentmihalyi, Miyali. (1991). *Flow: The Psychology of Optimal Experience.* Harper Perennial: New York, NY.

Ellis, Albert. (2001). *Feeling Better Getting Better, Staying Better.* Impact Publishers: Atascadero, CA.

Fredrickson, Barbara. (2009). Positivity: *Top Notch Research Reveals the 3:1 Ratio that will Change Your Life.* Three Rivers Press: New York, NY.

Fredrickson, Barbara. (2013). *LOVE 2.0: How Our Supreme Emotions Affects Everything We Feel, Think, Do and Become.* Hudson Street Press: New York, NY.

Fredrickson, Barbara. Positive Emotion. www.youtube.com/watch?v=Ds_9Df6dK7c.

Glasser, Howard. (2007). *All Children Flourishing: Igniting the Greatness of Our Children.* Nurtured Heart® Publications: Tucson, AZ.

Glasser, Howard. (2011). *Notching Up the Nurtured Heart Approach®.* The New Inner Wealth Initiative for Educators. Nurtured Heart® Publications: Tucson, AZ.

Glasser, Howard. (2009). *You Are Oprah: Igniting the Fires of Greatness.* Nurtured Heart® Publications: Tucson, AZ.

Kassay, Kim. (2010). The Importance of High Frustration Tolerance in Children. www.rebtinstitute.org/blog/2010/11/17/the-importance-of-high-frustration-tolerance-in-children/. Retrieved on 12/10/11.

Kassay, Kim. (2011). Helping Children Take Responsibility for Their Actions and Emotions. www.rebtinstitute.org/blog/2011/05/30/helping-children-take-responsibility-for-their-actions-and-emotions/. Retrieved on 12/10/11.

Knaus, Bill. Smart Recovery: *A Sensible Primer.*

Layous K, Nelson SK, Oberle E, Schonert-Reichl KA, Lyubomirsky S (2012). *Kindness Counts: Prompting Prosocial Behavior in Preadolescents Boosts Peer Acceptance and Well-Being.* PLoS ONE 7(12): e51380. doi:10.1371/journal.pone.0051380.

References

Editor: Frank Krueger, George Mason University/Krasnow Institute for Advanced Study.

Lyubomirsky, Sonja. (2007). *The How of Happiness: A New Approach to Getting the Life You Want.* Penguin Group: New York, NY.

Moles, Kerry. (2001). *The Teen Relationship Workbook: For Professionals Helping Teens to Develop Healthy Relationships and Prevent Domestic Violence.* Plainview, NY: Wellness Reproductions & Publishing, LLC.

Newmark, Sanford. (2010). *ADHD Without Drugs: A Guide to the Natural Care of Children with ADHD.* Brigham City, UT: Brigham Distributing.

Parks, Acacia & Seligman, Martin E.P. (2007). *8-Week Group Positive Psychotherapy (PPT) Manual Version 2.* Positive Psychology Center, University of Pennsylvania.

Peterson, Christopher & Seligman, Martin. (2004). *Character Strengths and Virtues: A Handbook and Classification.* Oxford University Press: New York, NY.

Pinker, Stephen. "Human Nature's Pathologist." nytimes.com/2011/11/29/ www.science/human-natures-pathologist.html?pagewanted=all Retrieved 11/30/11.

Rosenberg, Morris. (1989). *Society and the Adolescent Self-Image.* Revised edition. Middletown, CT: Wesleyan University Press.

Seligman, Martin. (2011). *Flourish: A Visionary New Understanding of Happiness and Well Being.* Free Press: New York, NY.

Seligman, Martin. (2003). *Authentic Happiness: Using the New Positive Psychology to Realize Your Potential for Lasting Fulfillment.* Free Press: New York, NY.

Venefica, Avia.

We have sent information about how we are using the self-esteem scale to:
The Morris Rosenberg Foundation
c/o Dept. Of Sociology
University of Maryland
2112 Art/Soc Building
College Park, MD 20742-1315

20237348R00136

Made in the USA
Charleston, SC
02 July 2013